INTRODUCING
ISSUES WITH
OPPOSING
VIEWPOINTS®

The Election Process

Noël Merino, *Book Editor*

GREENHAVEN PRESS
A part of Gale, Cengage Learning

GALE
CENGAGE Learning·

Detroit • New York • San Francisco • New Haven, Conn • Waterville, Maine • London

Elizabeth Des Chenes, *Director, Publishing Solutions*

For more information, contact:
Greenhaven Press
27500 Drake Rd.
Farmington Hills, MI 48331-3535
Or you can visit our Internet site at gale.cengage.com

For product information and technology assistance, contact us at

Gale Customer Support, 1-800-877-4253
For permission to use material from this text or product, submit all requests online at www.cengage.com/permissions

Further permissions questions can be e-mailed to permissionrequest@cengage.com

Articles in Greenhaven Press anthologies are often edited for length to meet page requirements. In addition, original titles of these works are changed to clearly present the main thesis and to explicitly indicate the author's opinion. Every effort is made to ensure that Greenhaven Press accurately reflects the original intent of the authors. Every effort has been made to trace the owners of copyrighted material.

Cover image © Andrey Burmakin/Shutterstock.com.

LIBRARY OF CONGRESS CATALOGING-IN-PUBLICATION DATA

The election process / Noël Merino, book editor
    p. cm. -- (Introducing issues with opposing viewpoints)
  Summary: "The Election Process: Introducing Issues with Opposing Viewpoints is a series that examines current issues from different viewpoints, set up in a pro/con format"--Provided by publisher.
 Includes bibliographical references and index.
 ISBN 978-0-7377-6276-1 (hardback)
 1. Elections--United States--Juvenile literature. I. Merino, Noël
JK1978.E44 2012
 324.60973--dc23
                                                    2012024249

Printed in the United States of America
1 2 3 4 5 6 7 16 15 14 13 12

Contents

Chapter 3: How Can the Election Process Be Improved?

Foreword

Indulging in a wide spectrum of ideas, beliefs, and perspectives is a critical cornerstone of democracy. After all, it is often debates over differences of opinion, such as whether to legalize abortion, how to treat prisoners, or when to enact the death penalty, that shape our society and drive it forward. Such diversity of thought is frequently regarded as the hallmark of a healthy and civilized culture. As the Reverend Clifford Schutjer of the First Congregational Church in Mansfield, Ohio, declared in a 2001 sermon, "Surrounding oneself with only like-minded people, restricting what we listen to or read only to what we find agreeable is irresponsible. Refusing to entertain doubts once we make up our minds is a subtle but deadly form of arrogance." With this advice in mind, Introducing Issues with Opposing Viewpoints books aim to open readers' minds to the critically divergent views that comprise our world's most important debates.

Introducing Issues with Opposing Viewpoints simplifies for students the enormous and often overwhelming mass of material now available via print and electronic media. Collected in every volume is an array of opinions that captures the essence of a particular controversy or topic. Introducing Issues with Opposing Viewpoints books embody the spirit of nineteenth-century journalist Charles A. Dana's axiom: "Fight for your opinions, but do not believe that they contain the whole truth, or the only truth." Absorbing such contrasting opinions teaches students to analyze the strength of an argument and compare it to its opposition. From this process readers can inform and strengthen their own opinions, or be exposed to new information that will change their minds. Introducing Issues with Opposing Viewpoints is a mosaic of different voices. The authors are statesmen, pundits, academics, journalists, corporations, and ordinary people who have felt compelled to share their experiences and ideas in a public forum. Their words have been collected from newspapers, journals, books, speeches, interviews, and the Internet, the fastest growing body of opinionated material in the world.

Introducing Issues with Opposing Viewpoints shares many of the well-known features of its critically acclaimed parent series, Opposing Viewpoints. The articles are presented in a pro/con format, allowing readers to absorb divergent perspectives side by side. Active reading questions preface each viewpoint, requiring the student to approach the material thoughtfully and carefully. Useful charts, graphs, and cartoons supplement each article. A thorough introduction provides readers with crucial background on an issue. An annotated bibliography points the reader toward articles, books, and websites that contain additional information on the topic. An appendix of organizations to contact contains a wide variety of charities, nonprofit organizations, political groups, and private enterprises that each hold a position on the issue at hand. Finally, a comprehensive index allows readers to locate content quickly and efficiently.

Introducing Issues with Opposing Viewpoints is also significantly different from Opposing Viewpoints. As the series title implies, its presentation will help introduce students to the concept of opposing viewpoints and learn to use this material to aid in critical writing and debate. The series' four-color, accessible format makes the books attractive and inviting to readers of all levels. In addition, each viewpoint has been carefully edited to maximize a reader's understanding of the content. Short but thorough viewpoints capture the essence of an argument. A substantial, thought-provoking essay question placed at the end of each viewpoint asks the student to further investigate the issues raised in the viewpoint, compare and contrast two authors' arguments, or consider how one might go about forming an opinion on the topic at hand. Each viewpoint contains sidebars that include at-a-glance information and handy statistics. A Facts About section located in the back of the book further supplies students with relevant facts and figures.

Following in the tradition of the Opposing Viewpoints series, Greenhaven Press continues to provide readers with invaluable exposure to the controversial issues that shape our world. As John Stuart Mill once wrote: "The only way in which a human being can make some approach to knowing the whole of a subject is by hearing what can be said about it by persons of every variety of opinion and studying all modes in which it can be looked at by every character of mind. No wise man ever acquired his wisdom in any mode but this." It is to this principle that Introducing Issues with Opposing Viewpoints books are dedicated.

Introduction

"Speech is an essential mechanism of democracy, for it is the means to hold officials accountable to the people. . . . The right of citizens to inquire, to hear, to speak, and to use information to reach consensus is a precondition to enlightened self-government and a necessary means to protect it."

—Justice Anthony Kennedy, *Citizens United v.*
Federal Election Commission (2010)

One of the most controversial issues regarding the US election process is the financing of campaigns. At the core of many concerns about campaign finance is the worry that money can have undue influence on the outcome of elections, threatening the democratic process. At the same time, many argue that money is simply a way for many people to exercise their First Amendment right to freedom of speech and that it need not be corrupting to the political process. Over the years, regulations of campaign finance have been passed; many of those regulations were eventually repealed or thrown out.

Up until the 1970s, there was little legislation that regulated the financing of campaigns. In 1971 Congress passed the Federal Election Campaign Act (FECA). FECA required reporting of campaign contributions and expenditures, and also limited spending on media advertisements. Also passed in 1971 was the Revenue Act, establishing a fund that allowed taxpayers to designate money to finance presidential elections. After the 1972 presidential elections, in which there were many documented campaign abuses, the impetus was created to establish an independent body to ensure compliance with the campaign finance laws. The 1974 amendments to FECA included the establishment of the Federal Election Commission (FEC), an independent regulatory agency that was founded in 1975, whose duties are "to disclose campaign finance information, to enforce the provisions of the law such as the limits and prohibitions on contributions, and to oversee the public funding of Presidential elections."[1]

Key provisions of the 1974 FEC amendments were challenged in *Buckley v. Valeo* (1976). The US Supreme Court in *Buckley* upheld campaign contribution limits but overturned campaign expenditure limits, claiming, "It is clear that a primary effect of these expenditure limitations is to restrict the quantity of campaign speech by individuals, groups and candidates. The restrictions . . . limit political expression at the core of our electoral process and of First Amendment freedoms." This important Supreme Court decision established that spending in campaigns was protected by the First Amendment to the US Constitution, which guarantees "Congress shall make no law . . . abridging the freedom of speech." The decision set the stage for allowing wealthy presidential candidates such as Ross Perot, Steve Forbes, and Mitt Romney to spend unlimited amounts of their own money in pursuit of the presidency.

In 2002 Congress made major revisions to FECA in the Bipartisan Campaign Reform Act (BCRA). The legislation prohibited national political party committees from raising or spending money not subject to federal limits and prohibited issue advocacy ads by corporations or organizations within sixty days of an election. In *Federal Election Commission v. Wisconsin Right to Life, Inc.* (2007), the US Supreme Court held that the prohibition on issue advocacy ads was unconstitutional when there was a reasonable interpretation of an ad as not promoting a specific candidate. And in *Citizens United v. Federal Election Commission* (2010), the court struck down the portions of the BCRA that limited political issue advocacy by corporations, again relying on the First Amendment, stating: "If the First Amendment has any force, it prohibits Congress from fining or jailing citizens, or associations of citizens, for simply engaging in political speech."

The *Citizens United* decision has profoundly changed the campaign-finance landscape by lifting restrictions on political expenditures for electioneering communications by corporations and unions. Republican Senate minority leader Mitch McConnell supported the decision: "For too long, some in this country have been deprived of full participation in the political process. With today's monumental decision, the Supreme Court took an important step in the direction of restoring the First Amendment rights of these groups." Conversely, Democratic US representative Leonard Boswell said of the *Citizens United* decision, "The Supreme Court's ruling today strikes at the very core of democracy in the United States by inflating the speech rights of large, faceless corporations to the same level of hard-working, everyday Americans."[2]

The debate over the *Citizens United* decision is far from over. Nonetheless, many campaign finance regulations still exist. As of 2012, individual contribution limits are capped at $2,500 per candidate with a biennial limit of $46,200 for all candidates and $70,800 to all political actions committees and political parties. Corporations and labor unions are prohibited from making direct contributions to candidates in federal elections but may now make unlimited expenditures in connection with federal elections as long as they are independent from the campaign. This disparate legal treatment of "hard" money and "soft" money is likely to continue to be a source of contention, causing some—including Representative Boswell—to call for a constitutional amendment to undo the *Citizens United* decision.

Because so much is at stake, the election process is fraught with controversy. Campaign finance is just one of the many issues that elicits a variety of viewpoints. Voter eligibility, voting equipment and vote-counting procedures, voter turnout, and voting systems are all issues that provoke diverse proposals for reform. A variety of viewpoints on many of these issues are included in *Introducing Issues with Opposing Viewpoints: The Election Process*.

Notes

1. Federal Election Commission, "About the FEC," www.fec.gov.
2. Quoted in Kasie Hunt, "John McCain, Russ Feingold Diverge on Court Ruling," *Politico*, January 21, 2010. www.politico.com/news/stories/0110/31810.html.

Chapter 1

Is the Election Process Fair and Inclusive?

A young woman casts her vote in a recent election. Most Americans consider the right to vote to be a sacred privilege.

Voter Fraud Is a Problem Affecting Fair Elections

"Not only is the risk of voter fraud real but . . . it could affect the outcome of a close election."

Conn Carroll

In the following viewpoint, Conn Carroll argues that voter fraud is a real concern. Carroll contends that the US Department of Justice is not adequately enforcing the law against voter fraud, and he urges people to be aware of such fraud and to report violations. Carroll claims that the right to vote is a fundamental right that needs to be protected from fraud since the temptation of fraud is inherent in the election process.

Carroll is a senior editorial writer for the *Washington Examiner*.

AS YOU READ, CONSIDER THE FOLLOWING QUESTIONS:

1. According to the author, what three felonies are committed when a noncitizen registers to vote and then votes?
2. Carroll claims that voter fraud is of particular concern in what kind of electoral races?
3. Is electioneering in the polling place allowed, according to Carroll?

V oter fraud happens. Just ask Olivia Alair, press secretary for the U.S. Department of Transportation. Alair was regional communications director for the 2008 election in Ohio under White House press secretary Robert Gibbs. In 2008, Alair and two other [Barack] Obama campaign staffers registered to vote in Ohio. The problem was that Alair did not live in Ohio and had no permanent plans to do so. By Ohio law, this made her ineligible to register. Only after this was made public did Alair and her cohorts send letters asking that their registrations be canceled. If the press had never made this public, would Alair have gone ahead and committed a felony by voting? Only she knows. But her cavalier attitude toward our nation's voting laws permeates the entire Obama administration.

Instances of Voter Fraud

In 2004, an immigrant illegally registered to vote in Putnam County, Tenn., and then voted illegally. This is a felony three times over! 18 U.S.C. § 1015(f) makes it illegal to claim you are a U.S. citizen in order to register to vote for any election; 18 U.S.C. § 611 prohibits a noncitizen from voting in an election where there is a federal candidate on the ballot; and 18 U.S.C. § 911 makes false claims of citizenship in general a felony. Instead of prosecution, the Obama administration sent the immigrant a letter asking him when he "discovered" that he was "not a United States Citizen." Protecting the ballot box was not their priority.

And the Tennessee case was not an isolated incident. Thanks to the U.S. Commission on Civil Rights, we now know that not protecting the ballot box from voter fraud is the official policy of the Obama Justice Department [DOJ]. Former American Civil Liberties Union attorney and current Justice Department employee Christopher Coates testified before the [commission] that: 1) Deputy Assistant Attorney General Julie Fernandes ordered DOJ attorneys only to enforce "traditional types of [voter intimidation] cases that

> **FAST FACT**
>
> The Criminal Division of the US Department of Justice is charged with overseeing the enforcement of federal laws that criminalize voter fraud and protect the integrity of the federal election process.

would provide political equality for racial and minority language voters;" and 2) Fernandes informed DOJ attorneys that it was the policy of the Obama administration not to enforce anti-voter fraud laws since Obama "was not interested in that type of issue, but instead interested in issues that pertained to voter access." Fernandes has never responded to these allegations.

Fraud in Close Elections

For most electoral races today, fraud will not be a factor. But there are some races where some will desperately cling to power in a close election. And that is where voting fraud is most likely to happen. The Heritage Foundation's voting law expert Hans von Spakovsky told Fox News: "Any place where we have very close elections, there's always going to be the potential there that voter fraud may make a difference, and that's where we are going to have to be really careful to be sure that doesn't happen."

Tennessee lawmakers confer in the statehouse. The state is but one of many that see multiple instances of voter fraud.

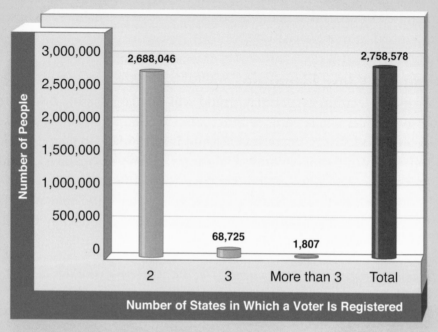

Voters Registered in More than One State

Number of People

3,000,000	2,688,046		2,758,578
2,500,000			
2,000,000			
1,500,000			
1,000,000			
500,000			
0		68,725	1,807

| 2 | 3 | More than 3 | Total |

Number of States in Which a Voter Is Registered

Taken from: Pew Center on the States, "Inaccurate, Costly and Inefficient: Evidence That America's Voter Registration System Needs an Upgrade," February 14, 2012.

In fact, voter fraud has already happened in [the November 2010] election. A Daytona Beach [Florida] City Commissioner was arrested for absentee ballot fraud just last week. In Troy, N.Y., Democrats on the city council have been ordered to supply DNA to prosecutors to be tested against absentee ballots and absentee ballot applications that were allegedly forged. And in Bucks County, Pa., a Democratic program intimidated some voters into needlessly, and sometimes fraudulently, applying for absentee ballots.

A Most Basic Civil Right

Federal law does allow for poll workers to assist the disabled and those who can't read English. But, if you see or hear a poll worker attempt to give unsolicited instructions to any voter (other than technical instructions), that is not allowed. Neither is any electioneering in or near the polling place, and promises of payments for voting of any kind (whether it be cash or free food) are also illegal. If you witness any of these activities, notify both the chief election official in their particular county or city, as well as the media to make sure that officials do something about it.

The right to vote in a free and fair election is the most basic civil right, on which depends all of the other rights of the American people protected by the Bill of Rights. Unfortunately, as long as elections put people into positions where they can make decisions about how much the government will spend, who will receive the money, and how the government will exercise its power, elections will be important enough to tempt some individuals to steal them. As the Supreme Court recognized when it upheld the constitutionality of Indiana's voter identification law in 2008, flagrant examples of voter fraud "have been documented throughout this Nation's history by respected historians and journalists." Those examples "demonstrate that not only is the risk of voter fraud real but that it could affect the outcome of a close election." Be on the look out to protect your most basic civil right today.

EVALUATING THE AUTHOR'S ARGUMENTS:

In this viewpoint Conn Carroll urges people to be on the lookout for voter fraud at the polls. How would Christopher Beam, author of the following viewpoint, respond to Carroll's suggestion?

Viewpoint
2

There Is No Evidence of Widespread Voter Fraud

Christopher Beam

"No one should believe that voter fraud is a widespread problem."

In the following viewpoint, Christopher Beam argues that there is no reason to think that extensive voter fraud is occurring. Beam contends that voter fraud allegations are politically charged and that the evidence shows that concerns about fraudulent voting are unfounded. Furthermore, he argues that there is little reason to think most people would risk getting caught for voter fraud.

Beam is a reporter for the online magazine *Slate*, where he covers politics.

AS YOU READ, CONSIDER THE FOLLOWING QUESTIONS:

1. According to the author, which political party has led the way in raising concerns about voter fraud?
2. Beam says that a crackdown on voter fraud from 2002 to 2007 yielded how many convictions?
3. What punishment do perpetrators of voter fraud risk, according to Beam?

Christopher Beam, "Fake the Vote: Why Would Anyone Commit Voter Fraud?," *Slate Online*, October 26, 2010. Slate.com. Copyright © 2010 by Slate Magazine. All rights reserved. Reproduced by permission.

A nother election, another round of voter fraud allegations.
Republicans and Democrats—also known as the voter-fraud police and the voter-fraud-police police—are already manning their stations [for the November 2010 elections]. David Norcross, chairman of the Republican National Lawyers Association says that attempts to commit voter fraud are under way. Michelle Malkin announced on Fox News on Monday [October 25, 2010] that "we are all voter-fraud police now." Dick Armey, chairman of FreedomWorks, attributed the Democratic lead among early ballot voters to the fact that there's "less ballot security" in areas where Democratic voters dominate.

Responding to Voter Fraud Suspicions

In response, Tea Party groups and other organizations on the right are recruiting poll monitors to make sure no shenanigans take place. A Tea Party group in St. Paul has even offered a $500 reward for information that leads to a successful prosecution for voter fraud. In

Shown here is a voter ID card. According to the author, although research shows no evidence of widespread voter fraud, conservatives continue to push for voter ID laws.

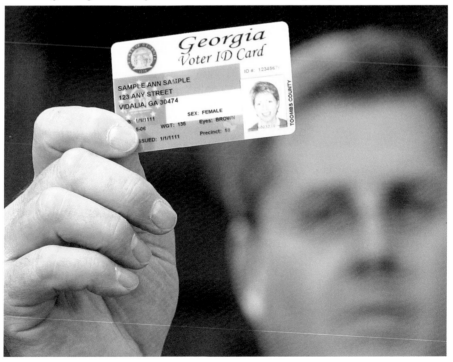

Milwaukee, billboards show people behind bars with the caption, "We Voted Illegally." Liberals, meanwhile, warn that conservative attempts to monitor the polls will intimidate voters and suppress turnout.

No one denies that ginning up fear about systematic voter fraud is an effective political tactic. It appeals to an electorate suspicious of government and helps delegitimize any victories that can be attributed to the over-enfranchisement of minorities, i.e. Democratic voters. But no one should believe that voter fraud is a widespread problem.

A Lack of Evidence

In 2002, the [George W.] Bush administration made cracking down on voter fraud a top priority. Five years later, the effort had yielded 86 convictions. About 30 convictions were linked to vote-buying schemes in races for small offices like sheriff or judge. Only 26 were attributable to individual voters, and most of those were misunderstandings about voter eligibility, such as felons who voted without knowing it was illegal. The prosecutions provided little evidence of organized fraud.

FAST FACT

The Help America Vote Act of 2002, which overhauled election law, required the US Election Assistance Commission (EAC) to study voter fraud and voter intimidation.

A 2007 study by the Brennan Center for Justice at New York University reached a similar conclusion. The vast majority of "fraud" cases, it found, were due to typographical errors in poll books and registration records, bad matches between voter databases (for example, you could be listed as John Smith in one database and John T. Smith in another), and voters registering at new addresses without deleting old registrations. Much of the alleged "voter fraud," it turns out, is just poorly filled out registration cards. And even if someone purposely files a fraudulent form by writing the name "Mickey Mouse," it doesn't affect the election. "Mickey Mouse doesn't vote," says Wendy Weiser of the Brennan Institute. Actual voter fraud—a voter pretending to be someone he's not—is, according to the study, less common than getting struck by lightning.

Federal Prosecutions of Voter Registration Fraud, 2002–2005

False Claim of Eligibility*	Outcome			
	Dismissed	Acquitted	Pled Guilty	Convicted
Noncitizen	4	1	3	13
Felon	4	1	3	2
False statement to grand jury about (11) voter-registration forgeries			1	
Conspiracy to submit false information on (2) voter-registration applications			1	
Total	8	2	8	15

*All but two of those charged with making false claims about their eligibility to register (two noncitizens who were convicted) were also charged with casting a false or fraudulent ballot, as reported above.

Taken from: US Department of Justice, Criminal Division, Public Integrity Section, *Election Fraud Prosecutions & Convictions, Ballot Access & Voting Integrity Initiative*, October 2002–September 2005. Source: LorraineC. Minnite, "The Politics of Voter Fraud," Project Vote, 2007.

A Crime That Makes No Sense

Perhaps the strongest evidence against claims of widespread voter fraud is that it would make no sense. Imagine what you'd have to do to perpetrate such a scheme. You'd first have to recruit a large number of voters willing to cooperate, each of whom would risk five years in prison and a $10,000 fine. Then you'd have to get them all registered, which would require fake IDs and mailing addresses. (The mailing address would have to be real so they could receive their registration cards.) The names and addresses would then get checked against a central state database. If the database fails to find a match, the voter's registration gets flagged for a follow-up check of their Social Security Number or driver's license number. Then on Election Day, they'd have to show their fake ID again and lie to a poll worker's face. At each point—registration, the database check, voting—they'd run the risk of getting caught. And the more people involved in the scheme, the more likely someone slips up. All it would take is one unlucky person for the whole plan to unravel.

And for what? The prospect of winning a few extra votes for a candidate you support simply isn't worth the risk of jail time. (This is especially true for illegal immigrants, who want to vote even if it means risking deportation, according to some anti-fraud crusaders.) And for large organizations, there are much better, safer, more efficient ways to steal an election, such as bribing an election official or tampering with voting machines. The punishment is just as harsh, but those methods require the participation of fewer people.

What's most confusing is how poll monitors would prevent fraud from occurring. Guidelines on "what to watch for" posted by the group Election Integrity Watch tell poll monitors to look out for buses, noncitizen voters, and voters with multiple ballots. But there's little they can do if voters simply create fake identities, which any large-scale systematic fraud would require.

There's nothing wrong with preventing voter fraud, just as there's nothing wrong with preventing alien attacks. First make sure the problem is worth your time.

EVALUATING THE AUTHOR'S ARGUMENTS:

In this viewpoint Christopher Beam says there is nothing wrong with preventing voter fraud, but he denies that widespread fraud exists. Based on his arguments, do you think he would agree with the following viewpoint by Risa L. Goluboff and Dahlia Lithwick, in which they claim that efforts to prevent voter fraud are racist, or would he deny this, agreeing instead with the position of Quin Hillyer in viewpoint 4 of chapter 1? Explain your answer.

Viewpoint

3

"Proponents of reforming the voting process seem blind to the fact that all of these seemingly neutral reforms hit poor and minority voters out of all proportion."

Efforts to Prevent Voter Fraud Discriminate Against Minorities

Risa L. Goluboff and Dahlia Lithwick

In the following viewpoint, Risa L. Goluboff and Dahlia Lithwick argue that new voting rules implemented to fight voter fraud are reminiscent of racist laws from the Jim Crow era. Goluboff and Lithwick claim that the reforms disproportionately impact minority and poor voters. In addition, the authors claim that the justifications given for the new rules echo the rationale for the disenfranchisement efforts of southern whites toward African Americans a century ago.

Goluboff is a professor of law and history at the University of Virginia and is the author of *The Lost Promise of Civil Rights.* Lithwick is a contributing editor at *Newsweek* and senior editor at *Slate.*

AS YOU READ, CONSIDER THE FOLLOWING QUESTIONS:
1. What law do the authors credit with preventing the worst kinds of minority vote suppression, such as those used in the nineteenth century?
2. Goluboff and Lithwick claim that use of the Australian, or secret, ballot kept many African American men from voting for what reason?
3. According to the authors, what is the underlying goal of the new voter restrictions?

A n elderly black woman in Tennessee can't vote because she can't produce her marriage certificate. Threatening letters blanket black neighborhoods warning that creditors and police officers will check would-be voters at the polls, or that elections are taking place on the wrong day. Thirty-eight states have instituted new rules prohibiting same-day registration and early voting on Sundays. All of this is happening as part of an effort to eradicate a problem that is statistically rarer than heavy-metal bands with exploding drummers: vote fraud.

The History of Minority Voter Suppression

Many commentators have remarked on the unavoidable historical memories these images provoke: They are so clearly reminiscent of the Jim Crow [racial segregation] era. So why shouldn't the proponents of draconian new voting laws have to answer for their ugly history?

Proponents of reforming the voting process seem blind to the fact that all of these seemingly neutral reforms hit poor and minority voters out of all proportion. (The Brennan Center for Justice estimates that while about 12 percent of Americans don't have a government-issued photo ID, the figure for African-Americans is closer to 25 percent, and in some Southern states perhaps higher.) The reason minorities are so much harder hit by these seemingly benign laws has its roots in the tragic legacy of race in this country. They still work because that old black man, born into Jim Crow in 1940, may have had no birth certificate because he was not born in a hospital because of poverty or discrimination. Names may have been misspelled on African-American birth certificates because illiterate midwives sometimes gave erroneous names.

It's true that the most egregious methods of minority vote suppression from the 19th century—the poll tax, the literacy test, the white primary—have disappeared. And we know (and can take some solace in the knowledge) that the worst of these indignities have not been recycled in the 21st century, in part because of the protections of the 1965 Voting Rights Act. But a look at the history of voting rights in this country shows that the current state efforts to suppress minority voting—from erecting barriers to registration and early voting to voter ID laws—look an awful lot like methods pioneered by the white supremacists from another era that achieved similar results.

The Rationale for Voting Rules

One device that was particularly effective was to require voters to register periodically and to make the registration process more elaborate than might seem necessary. (These rules were then often relaxed for white voters.) Residency requirements, both within and outside

Activists celebrate the end of Jim Crow laws in 1964. Opponents of voter ID cards say such IDs are an attempt to bring back Jim Crow laws and make it harder for minorities to vote.

the South, had the same, intended, effect of simply keeping people off the rolls. Under one law passed in Indiana in 1917, for example, the applicant had to specify the material his house was made of, his nearest neighbor's full name, and other proofs of residency. And of course then, as now, misinformation about registration and voting requirements, directed to some constituents and not to others, was a popular device for selective disfranchisement.

At first glance, it's hard to argue with the goal of reducing corruption and fraud in the election process. Even those who oppose the new provisions would agree that voter fraud is a bad thing. But as [investigative journalist] Ari Berman recently reminded us (again) [in "The GOP War on Voting," *Nation*, August 30, 2011], there is no evidence for widespread vote fraud, despite [George W.] Bush administration efforts to find some:

> After taking power, the Bush administration declared war on voter fraud, making it a "top priority" for federal prosecutors. In 2006, the Justice Department fired two U.S. attorneys who refused to pursue trumped-up cases of voter fraud in New Mexico and Washington, and [Bush deputy chief of staff] Karl Rove called illegal voting "an enormous and growing problem. . . ." [Yet] a major probe by the Justice Department between 2002 and 2007 failed to prosecute a single person for going to the polls and impersonating an eligible voter, which the anti-fraud laws are supposedly designed to stop. . . . A much-hyped investigation in Wisconsin, meanwhile, led to the prosecution of only .0007 percent of the local electorate for alleged voter fraud.

In short, if we want to fight imaginary problems, we'd be better off going after the scourge of exploding drummers.

Even more remarkable than the similarities of the techniques being used to suppress minority voting today is that the reasons for introducing all of these new rules echo the pretextual rationales of the Jim Crow era. These are the very same justifications white southerners offered for their disfranchisement efforts more than a century ago. As historian C. Vann Woodward put it in *Origins of the New South,* "Repugnance for corrupt elections was put forward everywhere as the primary reason for disfranchisement." The call for the Australian ballot—the secret ballot that would effectively disfranchise the more than half of African-American men who could not read in 1900 (not to mention the 20 percent of whites who would lose the vote if the tests were fairly administered)—was a call for a fair ballot, one free of the influence and corruption that it was thought would inevitably follow from allowing the uneducated to vote. Reformers concerned with fraud instituted the secret ballot in 38 states in the final 12 years of the 19th century—with northern whites as worried about immigrant "hordes" and the "inferior" races of new possessions in the Caribbean and Pacific as southern whites were about African-Americans.

The New Jim Crow Era

Of course, back then such claims were deeply bound up with white supremacy and the corrupt practices of white politicians jockeying for black or immigrant votes. And the anti-fraud rationale went hand-in-hand with explicit and open calls for white supremacy. No longer is it politically palatable to declare, as a Virginian [delegate R.L. Gordon] who did at the turn of the 20th century, that one intends "to disfranchise every negro that [one can] . . . and as few white people as possible." Now we simply have conservatives like [political activist] Paul Weyrich elliptically telling evangelicals in 1980: "I don't want everybody to vote."

Not only are the stated "anti-fraud" justifications for this new crop of voter restrictions the same as they were in 1890, but the underlying goal of these restrictions is also unchanged: to shape an electorate that will vote for particular kinds of politicians. In a country

> **FAST FACT**
>
> From the 1880s into the 1960s, a majority of American states enforced racial segregation through so-called Jim Crow laws (named after a black character in minstrel shows).

with hugely shifting demographics, that problem is as urgent as it was a century ago for so-called "reformers." In the Jim Crow era, the impulse for disenfranchisement came from the Democratic Party, which used new restrictions on black voters to become the Solid South. Today, it is the Republican Party capitalizing on the remnants of Jim Crow to restrict the votes of the poor and minority communities most likely to vote for Democrats. It is the same impulse we see when [former Republican US senator] Rick Santorum says that if Republicans could only eliminate

"Shouldn't that read 'voting rights?,'" cartoon by Steve Greenberg, www.CartoonStock.com. Copyright © by Steve Greenberg. Reproduction rights obtainable from www.CartoonStock.com. Reproduced by permission.

single mothers, more Republicans will be elected. It's a way of saying some voters simply count more than others. The Constitution is quite clear, at least where race is concerned, that the opposite is true.

Voting is a right, and when the state erects barriers to the exercise of fundamental rights, the means should match the stated ends. In the case of vote fraud we are attempting to eradicate a problem that doesn't exist with horribly expensive measures that will not fix it. In the process we are enshrining a revived Jim Crow.

EVALUATING THE AUTHOR'S ARGUMENTS:

In this viewpoint Risa L. Goluboff and Dahlia Lithwick contend that laws attempting to stop voter fraud are racist. From what they say here, are all laws that attempt to eliminate such fraud discriminatory, or only some of them? Explain your answer.

Efforts to Prevent Voter Fraud Are Not Racist

Quin Hillyer

"*If there is a partisan or ideological bent to conservative attempts to de-fang the Left's fraud snakes, it is born not of racial animus but of a legitimate need for protection of honest ballots.*"

In the following viewpoint, Quin Hillyer argues that measures attempting to stop voter fraud are not racist, as Democratic Party leaders have suggested. Hillyer claims that there is evidence of voter fraud, making it a legitimate target of voting reform. Furthermore, he claims that there is evidence that successful fraud tends to favor Democrats, which may explain why preventing fraud is a Republican cause that is fought by the Left.

Hillyer is a senior editor of the *American Spectator* and a senior fellow at the Center for Individual Freedom.

AS YOU READ, CONSIDER THE FOLLOWING QUESTIONS:
1. According to Hillyer, which two Democratic leaders charged that Republican attempts at voter fraud prevention are racist?
2. What firsthand example does Hillyer give in support of his view that even voter identification may not stop voter fraud?
3. The author insinuates that what presidential election was tainted by voter fraud?

Democratic National Committee [DNC] Chair Rep. Debbie Wasserman Schultz, Florida Democrat, has ripped the scab from a deep wound in American politics. The Left has spent years slinging at conservatives the calumny that we want to block access to the polls by minority groups. The charge is a vile slander. Yet in the space of just two weeks, DNC chiefs have twice gone public with the allegation—race-baiting for all they are worth—in a raw attempt to foment racial tension. Beneath the surface, it's also an attempt to provide a smokescreen for fraudulent voting.

Charges of Racism

Wasserman Schultz minced no words on June 5, [2011,] telling [journalist] Roland Martin that Republicans "want to literally drag us all the way back to Jim Crow laws and literally—and very transparently—block access to the polls to voters who are more likely to vote Democratic candidates than Republican candidates."

She was parroting former DNC Chair Donna Brazile, who on May 17 wrote in *USA Today* that "from coast to coast, the GOP is engaged in what appears to be a coordinated, expensive effort to block voters from the polls. The motivation is political—a cynical effort to restrict voting by traditionally Democratic-leaning Americans. In more than 30 states, GOP legislators are on the move. . . . What the GOP is attempting to do is change the rules of the game, leaving only their players on the field."

But when Wasserman Schultz turned the political explicitly into the racial, even she was quickly forced to acknowledge she had gone too far—only to repeat the slur right away: "Jim Crow was the wrong analogy to use. . . . But I don't regret calling attention to the efforts in a number of states with Republican dominated legislatures, including Florida, to restrict access to the ballot box for all kinds of voters, but particularly young voters, African Americans and Hispanic Americans."

According to the author, many Democrats, such as Representative Debbie Wasserman Schultz (pictured), accuse Republicans of seeking to block minority groups and young voters from having access to the polls.

The Worry About Illegal Voting

Brazile is complaining about legislative attempts to require voter ID at the polls, in order to fight illegal voting. The truth is, legislators have every reason to worry about vote fraud. Fraud is appallingly easy—perhaps even with identification. Federal motor-voter laws actually outlaw reasonable safeguards against shenanigans. I just saw first-hand how lax the standards are. On Tuesday [June 7], I transferred my driver's license from Virginia to Alabama. Not once was I asked to provide even a sliver of proof that I actually reside in Alabama, much less in the house I live in. I could have claimed any address I wanted, and gotten away with it.

People attempt illegal voting all the time. Fortunately, some get caught. At the Election Law Center blog, J. Christian Adams keeps track. On June 3, a couple was arrested for vote fraud in Rhode Island. On May 31, trial was set in Texas for a city councilman who falsified dozens of mail-in ballot applications. On May 24 in Mississippi, two people were sentenced for illegal voting. On May 20, there was a vote-fraud story from Wisconsin; on May 18, a different one from Mississippi. May 17, New Jersey; May 10, Ohio; May 3 in Florida; also May 3 in New York, and April 29 in East St. Louis. On the stories go, *ad infinitum*.

John Fund's *Stealing Elections* documents the problem at great length. Among the highlights was his report of the massive Wisconsin vote fraud in 2004, including "ineligible voters casting ballots, felons not only voting but working at the polls, transient college students casting improper votes, and homeless voters possibly voting more than once." Then there was the case of Ritzy Mekler, the springer spaniel registered to vote in St. Louis for eight years—which still wasn't as interesting as when *USA Today* reported that goldfish Princess Nudelman received registration materials in a Chicago suburb. The problem was, poor Princess was a cold fish—cold dead, that is.

> ## FAST FACT
>
> The now-defunct Association of Community Organizations for Reform Now (ACORN) came under fire in the 2008 presidential election over allegations of voter registration fraud.

The figures below show the percentages of Americans who thought that votes cast by people ineligible to vote would be a major problem in two recent election cycles.

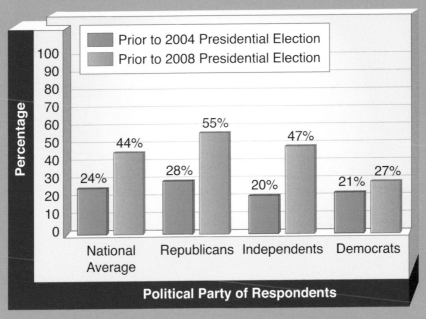

Taken from: Gallup Poll, October 14–16, 2004, and October 26–28, 2008.

The Political Gain from Voter Fraud

The simple fact is that, from [the now closed] ACORN [Association of Community Organizations for Reform Now] illegalities nationwide to massive abuses in Noxubee County, Miss., from mysteriously "discovered" ballots in a Washington State governor's race stretching all the way back to the manifest irregularities in Illinois and Texas that snatched the presidency for John F. Kennedy over Richard Nixon, illegal voting overwhelmingly tends to favor the political Left. If there is a partisan or ideological bent to conservative attempts to de-fang the Left's fraud snakes, it is born not of racial animus but of a legitimate need for protection of honest ballots. If Republicans are, in

Wasserman Schultz's words, trying to "block access to the polls to voters who are more likely to vote Democratic candidates," then it is only because illegal voters are more likely to vote for Democrats.

Those are "voters" whose access darn well ought to be blocked. Illegal aliens, dogs, dead people and dead goldfish have no business deciding who our public officials are.

EVALUATING THE AUTHOR'S ARGUMENTS:

In this viewpoint Quin Hillyer argues that illegal voters are more likely to vote for Democrats. How might Risa L. Goluboff and Dahlia Lithwick, authors of the preceding viewpoint, respond to Hillyer's claim?

Absentee Voting and Early Voting Are Important for Democracy

"The current block the vote efforts are occurring precisely at a time when history tells us that we should be extending the vote."

NAACP Legal Defense and Educational Fund and NAACP (National Association for the Advancement of Colored People)

In the following viewpoint, the NAACP (National Association for the Advancement of Colored People) and the NAACP Legal Defense and Educational Fund argue that the efforts underway to restrict early voting and absentee voting threaten voter participation in democracy. In addition, the authors contend that the measures limiting early and absentee voting disproportionately restrict participation by African Americans.

The NAACP works to eliminate race-based discrimination, and the NAACP Legal Defense and Educational Fund works toward this goal through litigation, advocacy, and public education.

AS YOU READ, CONSIDER THE FOLLOWING QUESTIONS:
1. According to the authors, on Election Day in 2008, what percentage of African American voters reported waits of half an hour or more?
2. The authors claim that Florida's reduction of early voting days could reduce total hours of early voting by as much as how many hours?
3. According to the authors, what voting restriction has been proposed in New Jersey?

A number of states have passed or considered measures that impede the actual casting of ballots by registered voters by placing new restrictions on the early and absentee voting processes. In 2011, five states (Florida, Georgia, Maine, Tennessee, and West Virginia) imposed new restrictions on early and absentee voting.

The Need for Early and Absentee Voting

Getting to the polls on Election Day is difficult for many voters. Many working individuals cannot afford to take time off of work (or simply lack the flexibility to be able to), low-income voters often lack easy access to transportation to the polls, the elderly and disabled may be unable to travel to the polls, and students and active service members may be absent from their voting precincts on Election Day.

> **FAST FACT**
>
> Oregon and Washington are the only two states that vote totally by mail, where a ballot is automatically mailed to every eligible voter prior to the election and then mailed back or dropped off by the voter.

To assist those voters who cannot reach polls on Election Day itself, almost all states provide some alternative to the traditional in-person, precinct-based Election Day method for casting a ballot. These alternatives usually involve a version of early, and/or absentee, voting.

Whether because of a lack of transportation or an inflexible work schedule, or because of long lines and waiting periods to vote on

Election Day (in 2008, 27% of African-American voters reported waits half an hour or more, as compared to only 11% of white voters), voters of color have been more likely to take advantage of the flexibility provided by these additional voting days.

Nevertheless, in the 2011 legislative cycle, bills were introduced in ten states to reduce early or absentee voting periods, with such bills passing in five states: Florida (enacted, subject to preclearance), Georgia (enacted), Maine (enacted), Maryland (pending but with unfavorable committee report), Nevada (no further action allowed), New Mexico (defeated), North Carolina (pending), Ohio (enacted subject to voter referendum), Tennessee (various bills enacted), and West Virginia (enacted).

Efforts to Reduce Early Voting in Florida

Highlights of these efforts include:

- *Florida's elimination of the first week of early voting:* Florida has enacted a bill that reduces the number of early voting days from fourteen to eight days. The bill also gives local supervisors of elections discretion over early voting hours, changing the hours that early voting sites must operate from a mandatory eight hours per day (other than weekends), to a discretionary range of six to twelve hours per day. As a result, the change not only eliminates the first week of early voting in Florida, but it also makes possible a reduction in total hours of early voting from a mandatory 96 hours to a minimum of only 48 hours.

  In the 2008 election, over 2.6 million votes were cast during Florida's early in-person voting period, accounting for an estimated 31.25% of all ballots cast.

  This change will inflict particularly harsh burdens on minority communities, who rely heavily on early voting periods to cast their ballots. During the 2008 general election, African Americans were 22% of voters during the first week of early voting in Florida statewide, despite being only 13% of the Florida electorate. Overall, 54% of Florida's African-American voters in 2008 voted at early voting sites.

- *Florida's elimination of early voting on the Sunday before Election Day:* Florida also eliminated early voting on the last Sunday before Election Day, a day on which African-American churches in Florida have traditionally conducted a sizeable portion of their election assistance efforts. One such example is the "Soul to the Polls" effort, in which churches encourage their congregants, after fulfilling their spiritual duties at church, to discharge their civic responsibilities, by organizing transportation from Sunday services directly to the election booth. African Americans comprised one-third of the entire statewide turnout on the last Sunday before the 2008 election.

Although not all of Florida's counties currently offer early voting on this last Sunday, those counties that do—Miami-Dade, Duval, Palm Beach, Broward (in 2008)—are urban counties that have among the largest African-American populations in the state.

Florida's law remains subject to review under Section 5 of the Voting Rights Act.

Voting Restrictions in Georgia and Ohio

- *Georgia's reduction of the early voting period from 45 days to 21 days:* Reversing its pre-2008 election decision to expand early in-person voting from one week to 45 days before the election, Georgia has returned to a shortened early voting period of only 21 days.

  Like the shortening of early voting in Florida, this change will disproportionately affect voters of color. According to a Pew Center on the States survey of voters in three Georgia counties, more than 60% of African Americans who voted in the 2008 general election did so during the early period, as compared to less than half of white voters. As a result, African Americans cast 35% of all early ballots, even though they comprised only 30% of those eligible to vote in the general election.

  In addition, African Americans voted early in the 45-day period—a portion of the early voting window that has since been eliminated—casting almost 40% of all the ballots during that time.

- *Ohio's return to 2004 election rules:* Ohio is reversing many of the voting conveniences introduced after the 2004 general election, when the nation watched while Ohioans in many counties waited up to ten hours at the polls.

  Among these reversals is a reduction in Ohio's 35-day early voting period. In 2008, approximately 30% of all Ohio voters cast their ballots during the early voting period. As a result, despite record turnout, 2008 did not suffer a reprise of the long waits at the polls witnessed in 2004.

Ohio's newly-shortened voting period signals a return to the ten-hour waits from 2004, particularly in urban areas where minority communities are concentrated, and where the proportion of early voters is as high as 40% in places like Franklin County. The changes to early voting also include a ban on in-person voting

The NAACP argues that restricting absentee and early balloting threatens minority voters' participation in democracy.

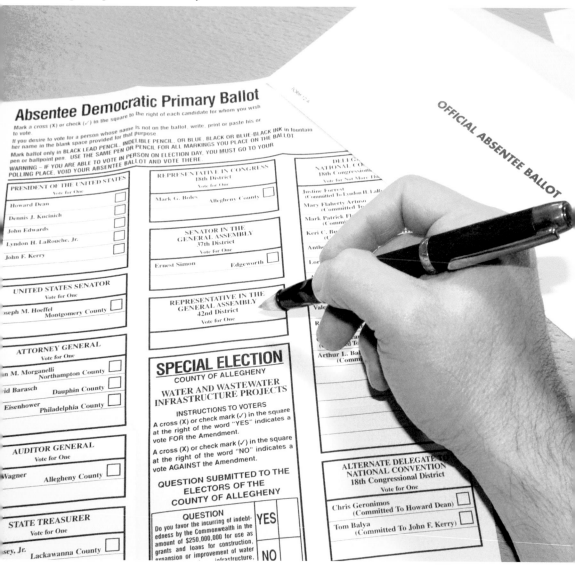

on Sundays. As one commentator notes, this particular ban, as in Florida, is "a transparent effort to limit voting by the African American community—whose members often come to vote in groups after church on Sunday." . . .

Other Restrictions on Early and Absentee Voting

State legislators have also proposed other creative methods to restrict access to these alternative methods of voting:

- Texas legislators introduced a bill that will omit early voting locations from official notices of a general or special election.

- As part of Ohio's recent overhaul of its voting system, Ohio Secretary of State Jon Husted sought to prohibit counties from mailing unsolicited absentee-ballot applications to voters and including prepaid return postage. These practices were employed by Franklin (Columbus), Cuyahoga (Cleveland), and Hamilton (Cincinnati) counties—the counties with the largest African-American populations by number and percentage—in past elections.

- A New Jersey bill would end no-excuse absentee voting.

Proponents of early voting restrictions argue that these measures provide needed cost savings, but the evidence indicates that these efforts will actually increase costs. In North Carolina, for example, the State Election Board found that cuts to early voting will increase expenses because the reduction would require the state to create new election precincts and add voting machines in order to handle the surge of voters now forced to vote on Election Day. At the same time, the cuts would reduce the flexibility early voting allows to allocate equipment and staff. . . .

Democracy in America is contested, as historian Alexander Keyssar has observed. It is characterized by periods of progress and retrenchment. As Keysaar notes, most of the American expansions in voting have occurred following periods of war when the reality of scores of returning service members has stimulated a conversation about the deeper ideals to which we are committed as a nation. Thus, the current block the vote efforts are occurring precisely at a time when history tells us that we should be extending the vote. With your steadfast commitment we can resist the anti-democratic efforts and extend the vote to more Americans. Our "more perfect union" depends upon it.

In this viewpoint the NAACP Legal Defense and
Educational Fund and NAACP (National Association for
the Advancement of Colored People) claim that measures
limiting early and absentee voting disproportionately
restrict participation by African Americans. Given this
concern, do you think the authors would agree with the
position of Risa L. Goluboff and Dahlia Lithwick in viewpoint 3 of this chapter? Why or why not?

Viewpoint

6

Extensive Absentee Voting Is Not Good for Democracy

"It won't be good for democracy if a flood of absentee ballots means the country will have to endure a slew of lawsuits and recounts."

John H. Fund

In the following viewpoint, John H. Fund argues that the increase in absentee voting has compromised the democratic process. Fund claims that absentee voting can cause delays in results, leading to uncertainty that can last weeks, and he denies that it improves voter turnout. He contends that absentee voting is more susceptible to fraud and coercion than secret voting at polling places, and he maintains there is a need for further safeguards and restrictions to reduce these new risks.

Fund is a senior editor of the *American Spectator* and the author of the book *Stealing Elections*.

AS YOU READ, CONSIDER THE FOLLOWING QUESTIONS:

1. Fund criticizes early voting by drawing what analogy?
2. Why does absentee voting make it easier to commit election fraud, according to Fund?
3. According to the author, what group found that local election officials have become careless in handling absentee ballots?

This year more voters than ever will cast ballots before Election Day. The result may be that in a world where everything seems to move faster we will get final election results later than ever. It's possible we won't know which party controls either house of Congress for days or even weeks because of all the disputes and delays caused by absentee ballots.

More than 30 states now allow anybody to cast an absentee vote. Several other states also allow early voting at government buildings or even grocery stores. This year, it's expected that nearly one in three Americans will vote before Election Day. For people who can't make it to the polls, absentee ballots are necessary.

But for others voting early is like judging the winner of a 15-round boxing match in the 16th round.

If control of Congress hinges on a few close races, don't expect to know the final outcome on Election Night. While early votes cast on electronic machines are easily integrated into the totals from traditional polling places, paper absentee ballots are typically counted only after the others.

In some super-tight races, a flood of absentee ballots could delay the results for weeks. "Any time you have more paper ballots cast outside polling places, the more mistakes and delays you're likely to have," Bill Gardner, New Hampshire's Democratic secretary of state, told me.

In Washington State, absentee ballots were the main reason that two recent statewide contests, for Senate in 2000 and governor in 2004, went into overtime. Democrat Maria Cantwell had to wait weeks to learn she had squeaked out a 2,200-vote plurality at a time when control of the U.S. Senate was in doubt. "Can anyone say it was a good thing the country had to wait until December 1 to learn the U.S. Senate would be tied?" asked John Carlson, a Seattle talk-show host.

FAST FACT

According to the US Election Assistance Commission, in the 2010 election, only 1 percent of absentee ballots were rejected as invalid—a third of these because the deadline had passed.

Opponents of early and absentee voting say that the results of tight races may be delayed for weeks as a result of the time needed to count those ballots.

Supporters of absentee voting insist that it increases turnout. But that's simply not the case. Curtis Gans, the director of the Center for the Study of the American Electorate, says that "academic studies all show that easy absentee voting decreases or has no effect on turnout."

Oregon has gone so far as to abolish polling places. Everyone votes by mail. But Melody Rose, political science professor at Portland State University, reports, "Voter turnout in Oregon looks much more like that of states with old-fashioned voting booths."

It's certainly true that voters like no-excuses absentee voting for its convenience. But it comes at a price. Absentee voting makes it easier to commit election fraud, because the ballots are cast outside the supervision of election officials. "By loosening up the restrictions on absentee voting they have opened up more chances for fraud,"

Damon Slone, a former West Virginia election fraud investigator, told the *New York Times*.

Absentee voting also corrupts the secret ballot. Because an absentee ballot is "potentially available for anyone to see, the perpetrator of coercion can ensure it is cast 'properly,' unlike a polling place, where a voter can promise he will vote one way but then go behind the privacy curtain and vote his conscience," notes John Fortier, a scholar at the American Enterprise Institute, in his book *Absentee and Early Voting*. Melissa Rimel, the president and founder of Colorado's Women Against Domestic Violence, recalls how she once was not even allowed to get the mail without her husband first going through it. She says that even if she would have been allowed to fill out a ballot it would have been done under the control of her abusive husband.

The need for safeguards against absentee fraud was underscored this year in Bell, California (pop. 40,000), where officials were forced out of office after it was found they were being paid outrageous salaries and pensions. City manager Robert Rizzo was not only paid $1.5 million, but also due a $600,000-a-year pension.

The scam was aided by having Bell officials take advantage of Bell's low voter turnout to commit ballot fraud. In 2005, fewer than 400 voters cast ballots—two-thirds of them absentee—in a special election that cleared the way for city council members to dramatically boost their own salaries.

Four voters told the *Los Angeles Times* that city officials walked door-to-door urging them to vote absentee. One later was counted as voting absentee even though she said she never filled out a ballot. Two other voters said local council members had personally collected their ballots for delivery, a violation of state law. In addition, a retired Bell police officer has identified at least 19 people he says voted but were either dead or living outside the country. He has provided a statement to Los Angeles prosecutors, who have opened an investigation.

The 2001 National Commission on Federal Election Reform, a bipartisan group co-chaired by the late Gerald Ford and Jimmy Carter, found that local election officials have grown sloppy in handling absentee ballots. "Most states do not routinely check signatures either on applications or on returned ballots, just as most states do not verify signatures or require proof of identity at the polls," noted John Mark Hansen, director of research for the commission's report.

John Fortier of AEI has some suggestions on how to retain the convenience of pre-Election Day voting but with a lower risk of fraud and intimidation. He suggests that states expand hours at polling places for early voting, but only during the 10 days before the election. New computer software can be used to match signatures on absentee ballots with registration records and flag those that raise concerns. States could require that every voter enclose a fingerprint or photocopy of some form of identification, not necessarily a photo ID.

If present trends continue, we will become a nation in which half of us vote on Election Day and the other half . . . well, whenever. While that may not bother some people, it won't be good for democracy if a flood of absentee ballots means the country will have to endure a slew of lawsuits and recounts that could delay the final results of next month's elections for weeks. Election Day could become Election Month before we know who will control the new Congress.

EVALUATING THE AUTHOR'S ARGUMENTS:

In this viewpoint John H. Fund uses quotes to bolster his argument. Make a list of people Fund quotes from and analyze their credentials. What impact do these quotes have on your opinion of Fund's argument?

Chapter 2

How Does Money Affect the Election Process?

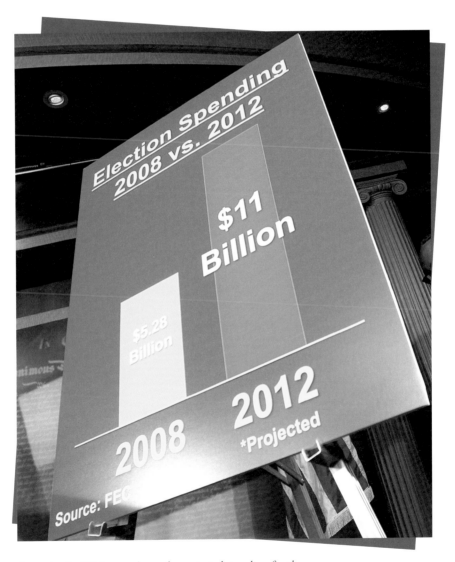

A sign in the US Senate shows the projected spending for the 2012 elections. Democrats have announced legislation intended to blunt the effects of the Citizens United v. Federal Election Commission *Supreme Court decision.*

The Supreme Court Was Correct to Overturn Limits on Corporate Campaign Advertising

"The [Supreme Court] decision actually sets the right example. By limiting government power, it protects our freedom."

Will Wilkinson

In the following viewpoint, Will Wilkinson argues that the US Supreme Court's decision in *Citizens United v. Federal Election Commission* (2010)—which ruled that the First Amendment protects the rights of corporations to spend money on political campaign advertising without limits—was the correct one. Wilkinson claims that progressives view this as a bad decision because they wrongly believe that corporations are evil, that special interests work primarily by influencing elections, and that government power should be used to balance corporate power. Instead, he concludes that the decision protects free speech and freedom.

Wilkinson is a writer who blogs about American politics for the *Economist.* His work has appeared in numerous publications.

AS YOU READ, CONSIDER THE FOLLOWING QUESTIONS:
1. For liberals, democracy is the embodiment of what ideal, according to Wilkinson?
2. As reported by the author, how much was spent on federal lobbying in 2009?
3. Wilkinson argues that government can only be the countervailing force to unequal citizen power if it is not already doing what?

When the Supreme Court overturned campaign finance law in *Citizens United v. Federal Election Commission* last month [January 2010], civil libertarians and free-speech enthusiasts applauded. The ruling threw out limits on corporate "independent expenditures" on campaign advertising—the case in point being a hatchet-job documentary on [former presidential candidate] Hillary Clinton produced by a non-profit corporation called Citizens United. Government censorship of political documentaries certainly seems to violate the very sinews of the First Amendment. "Congress shall make no law . . . abridging the freedom of speech" isn't very ambiguous, after all.

So I was caught off-guard when MSNBC's Keith Olbermann called the *Citizens United* decision "a Supreme Court-sanctioned murder of what little democracy is left in this democracy." When others followed with similar howls of wounded outrage, I became aware of a gap in my understanding of the progressive Left. I suddenly realized that free speech for big business is to the Left what due process for alleged terrorists is to the Right: an unbearable burden that threatens freedom itself.

The Liberal Ideal of Equal Freedom
For most progressives, democracy is more than a mere instrument for throwing the bums out. Democracy is instead the embodiment

US solicitor general Elena Kagan (now a US Supreme Court justice) argues in the Citizens United v. Federal Election Commission *case in the Supreme Court on September 9, 2009. The court's subsequent decision resulted in a sweeping reversal of campaign finance laws.*

of the liberal ideal of equal freedom. This sacred ideal is threatened, progressives argue, by concentrations of wealth that enable inequalities in political voice. If victory in the public sphere is determined by the size of one's megaphone, then wealthy interests with large megaphones will capture the system and rig it to their permanent advantage. Consequently, megaphones must be regulated to ensure an equitable democratic process.

The case for regulation seems even stronger to [journalist and social activist] Naomi Klein–style progressives, who fear the mind-warping powers of Madison Avenue [advertisers]. According to this line of thought, advertising is more hypnotic than informative, capable of seeding innocent minds with alien, false desires.

Thus for many progressives, the struggle for control of the mass media is a de facto struggle for democracy. If corporations are allowed to run riot over the airwaves, if commercial speech is not tightly controlled, we will lose our autonomy both as individuals and as a democratic people. Our public deliberations will be distorted by ideas that serve exclusive interests, and our puny individual voices will be drowned out by corporate foghorns.

But here's the progressive conundrum: Unless measures to reduce inequalities of voice have already been built into the system, our compromised democratic process will deliver government that reflects and reinforces them.

Given the difficulty of using a broken system to fix itself, progressives have labored for generations to establish a corrective legal framework that would put a thumb on the scales and tilt the balance of persuasive power toward plain people and away from corporations. The trouble is, the First Amendment is written in stubbornly plain language. By honoring the simple letter of that law, the *Citizens United* decision dealt a crushing blow to this progressive project, leaving them wailing as if all were lost.

The Flawed Progressive Analysis

But all is not lost—even for progressives. Because the analysis driving their outrage is badly flawed.

First, progressives mischaracterize the nature of corporations. Corporations are not essentially villainous agglomerations of money and power. They are a convenient form of social organization that enables large numbers of people to undertake cooperative endeavors. Nonprofit corporations, like Citizens United or the ACLU [American Civil Liberties Union], provide individuals the opportunity to amplify their lone voices in harmony with like-minded others. Meanwhile, for-profit corporations are little more than lenders' co-ops—a way for people to pool their resources to finance what look to be profitable lines of business. It is true that managers of corporations can—and do—take advantage of their owners and creditors. But there is a staggering number and diversity of for-profit corporations, and most of them, most

> **FAST FACT**
>
> In a five-to-four decision, the US Supreme Court held in *Citizens United v. Federal Election Commission* (2010) that the First Amendment prohibits government from placing limits on independent spending for political purposes by corporations and unions.

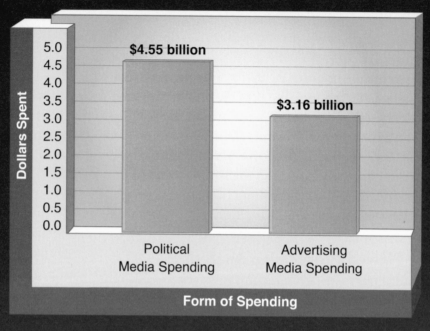

$4.55 billion

$3.16 billion

Dollars Spent

5.0
4.5
4.0
3.5
3.0
2.5
2.0
1.5
1.0
0.5
0.0

Political
Media Spending

Advertising
Media Spending

Form of Spending

Taken from: PQ Media, *Political Campaign Media Spending, 2010*, 2010.

of the time, do right by their stakeholders. Moreover, very few ever get involved in electoral politics in a significant way.

Which points to a second progressive error: the tendency to fixate on the high drama of elections rather than the more mundane processes by which corporate and other special interests actually do rig legislation and regulation in their favor. A single lobbyist with a good friend in the right place can deliver more to a special interest than many millions spent on campaign advertising. In 2009, $3.47 billion was spent on federal lobbying—a large sum, certainly, but not when you consider that the stimulus bill alone dispensed nearly $800 billion in public funds.

The Use of Government Power

But the granddaddy of all progressive errors—the one that breeds all others—is the assumption that greater government power can rectify the problem of unequal citizen power. Government can only act as a "countervailing force" in this regard if it is not acting already to serve corporate and special interests. But it is. That is why new government powers merely augment, rather than offset, the already disproportionate power of entrenched interests.

The biggest, baddest corporations, unions, and special interests already use government to exert power on their behalf. With the heft of the state behind them, they can swing sweetheart deals (witness earmarks) and they can foil upstart competitors (through regulation) who might otherwise eat their lunch. A government unhindered by limits retains the discretion to pick winners. A government that can make or break great fortunes invites a bruising and wasteful competition for its favor. It cannot be surprising, then, that those with the most—thus most to lose—assiduously seek favor from the state. It should not be surprising that those with powerful Washington connections are handsomely compensated by big special interests. And it should not be surprising when the well-connected exploit their relationships with people in power in the same way they maximize any other valuable asset.

Progressives are right to worry about corporatist government. But they locate the problem in the wrong place, which is why their proposed solutions repeatedly miss the target. It would be a great tragedy for democracy if a commonsense reading of the First Amendment's protection of free speech truly undermined democratic freedom. Thankfully, it does not. Ultimately, the *Citizens United* case will change very little about how our political system works. Election-season speech was never the chief means by which special interests did their dirty work. But in some modest measure, the decision actually sets the right example. By limiting government power, it protects our freedom.

EVALUATING THE AUTHOR'S ARGUMENTS:

In this viewpoint Will Wilkinson says that advertising during election season is not the primary way that special interests rig legislation and regulation. Does this position support his conclusion that removing limits from corporate political speech is the right decision? Why or why not?

The Supreme Court Erred in Overturning Limits on Corporate Campaign Advertising

"Citizens United vs. the Federal Election Commission . . . *will likely go down in history as one of the Supreme Court's most egregious exercises of judicial activism.*"

Thomas E. Mann

In the following viewpoint, Thomas E. Mann argues that the US Supreme Court's decision in *Citizens United v. Federal Election Commission* (2010)—ruling that the First Amendment protects the rights of corporations to spend money on political campaign advertising without limits—was an incorrect one. Mann warns that the decision could have a profound impact on elections and policy.

Mann is the W. Averell Harriman Chair and a Senior Fellow in Governance Studies at the Brookings Institution. He is coauthor of *The Broken Branch: How Congress Is Failing America and How to Get It Back on Track.*

AS YOU READ, CONSIDER THE FOLLOWING QUESTIONS:

1. As Mann reports, which US Supreme Court justice wrote the majority opinion in *Citizens United v. Federal Election Commission* (2010)?
2. What four legal means of having political impact does the author identify as having been used by corporations prior to the *Citizens United* decision?
3. Mann suggests that over the long haul, individuals do what to balance the political spending by corporations?

The 5–4 conservative majority decision in *Citizens United vs. the Federal Election Commission* that struck [down] many decades of law and precedent will likely go down in history as one of the Supreme Court's most egregious exercises of judicial activism.

An Immodest Decision

In spite of its imperative to rule on "cases and controversies" brought to the Court, to defer to the legitimate lawmaking authority of the Congress and other democratically elected legislatures, and to not allow simple disagreement with past judicial decisions to overrule precedent (*stare decisis*), the [Chief Justice John] Roberts Court ruled unconstitutional the ban on corporate treasury funding of independent political campaigns.

The Court reached to make new constitutional law by ordering a re-argument of a minor case that itself raised no direct challenge to the laws and precedents that it ultimately overruled; dismissed the legitimacy of laws enacted over a century by Congress and state legislatures; equated the free speech protections of individuals and corporations in spite of countless laws and precedents that insisted on meaningful differences; and provided not a shred of evidence of new conditions or harmful effects that justified imposing their own ideological preferences on a body of settled law and social tradition.

The decision makes a mockery of Chief Justice Roberts' pious statements during his confirmation hearing that he embraced judicial modesty and constitutional avoidance. His concurring decision to respond to his critics was defensive and lame.

Justice [John Paul] Stevens' caustic dissent eviscerating the majority opinion penned by Justice [Anthony] Kennedy and the Roberts' concurrence will likely be featured in legal journals and classes for decades to come.

The Impact of the Ruling

To be sure, *Citizens United* is not the first sign that the Roberts Court is dead set on deregulating campaign finance. Previous decisions have pointed in this direction and more are certain to follow.

How as a consequence are campaign finance practices likely to change? And what options exist for those who seek to limit or counter the anticipated fallout?

An immediate flood of corporate spending in federal and state campaigns is possible but uncertain. CEOs [chief executive officers] of some major corporations are wary of entering the political thicket in so transparent a fashion for fear of alienating customers and shareholders. Legal means already existed prior to this decision (PACs [political action committees, which are lobbying organizations], communications within the corporate family, issue ads, contributions to trade associations such as the Chamber of Commerce) to play a significant role in elections.

Privately controlled companies led by individuals with strong ideological and partisan motivations are most likely to take advantage of the new legal environment but they could already act without restraint as individuals. Perhaps the greatest impact will flow from the threat of corporate independent spending campaigns for or against officeholders whose position on issues before federal and state governments is important to their corporate interests. This could corrupt the policy process without any dollars actually being spent. It will be some time before we are able to gauge the real impact of *Citizens United*.

FAST FACT

Justice John Paul Stevens wrote in his dissent in *Citizens United v. Federal Election Commission* (2010), "A democracy cannot function effectively when its constituent members believe laws are being bought and sold."

Do you support or oppose the recent ruling by the US Supreme Court that says corporations and unions can spend as much money as they want to help political candidates win elections?

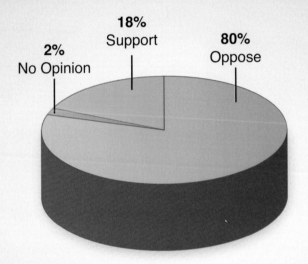

2%
No Opinion

18%
Support

80%
Oppose

Taken from: ABC News/*Washington Post* poll, February 4–8, 2010.

Ways of Countering the Ruling

In the meantime, Congress and legislatures in states with corporate prohibitions on their books will search for means of limiting or countering the ruling. Measures being considered are bans on political spending by corporations that have foreign ownership, government contracts or registered lobbyists or ones that have received federal bailout funds, strengthened disclosure, and requirements for shareholder approval of corporate political spending.

Most of these steps might be difficult to enact and even tougher to defend before post–*Citizens United* courts.

Over the longer haul, a more promising strategy is to fashion policy to encourage the proliferation of small donors to balance the political

A Super PAC is a political-action committee that is allowed to raise and spend unlimited amounts of money, provided that it has no direct contact with any candidate or political party. Here, senators Chuck Schumer (left) and Al Franken show how much secret money goes to just one Super PAC. The Citizens United *Supreme Court decision ruled such secret contributions to be legal.*

spending by corporations. In addition, politicians and citizen groups can speak and organize in a way that increases the costs to corporations who might otherwise avail themselves of this new opportunity. Large institutional and individual investors offended by the prospect of corporate treasuries being raided for political campaigns at the direction of top management might be persuaded to lead shareholder campaigns against such activities.

A radical conservative Supreme Court majority cavalierly decided to redress an alleged shortage of corporate political speech in American democracy. If, as I suspect, most Americans are bewildered and dismayed by that decision, their best recourse is to use their numbers and organizing energies to ensure that individual speech is not drowned by the trillions of dollars of corporate assets.

EVALUATING THE AUTHOR'S ARGUMENTS:

In this viewpoint Thomas E. Mann suggests that privately controlled companies led by individuals are most likely to take advantage of the repealed limits on campaign spending. In what way would Will Wilkinson, author of the preceding viewpoint, use the First Amendment to defend such spending as a form of free speech?

Reforms to Remove the Influence of Big Money on Elections Are Necessary

"It's urgent for Congress to curb the influence of money in our elections."

Nick Nyhart and David Donnelly

In the following viewpoint, Nick Nyhart and David Donnelly argue that politicians have become too focused on raising money for elections instead of serving the interests of their constituents. The authors contend that reform is needed to take the money out of the system, and they claim that this sentiment is shared by the vast majority of Americans.

Nyhart is executive director and Donnelly the national campaigns director of the Public Campaign Action Fund, a nonprofit, nonpartisan organization dedicated to improving America's campaign finance laws.

AS YOU READ, CONSIDER THE FOLLOWING QUESTIONS:
1. The authors charge that the senators backing repeal of the financial reform bill passed in 2010 took how much money in campaign contributions from Wall Street?
2. How many members of Congress cosponsored the 2011 reintroduction of the Fair Elections Now Act, according to Nyhart and Donnelly?
3. According to the authors, what fraction of voters thought the money spent in the 2010 elections posed a threat to fairness and the ability to get results?

As Congressional and White House negotiators wrestled with competing budget plans to avoid a government shutdown, no sane observer believed they'd put corporate tax loopholes—the kind large enough for a $3.2 billion rebate for profitable, and politically powerful, General Electric [GE]—on the chopping block. It was easy to see why: as negotiators preserved GE's tax breaks and cut programs for the poor, power-brokers in Washington operated at breakneck speed, attending the 122 fundraising events for lawmakers over the final few days of March [2011], as chronicled by the Sunlight Foundation's PoliticalPartyTime.org.

The Impact of Big Money

Unfortunately, it's a story Americans know all too well. For three elections in a row—2006, 2008 and 2010—we've sent people to change the way Washington works, only to see Washington's big-money culture change them. Those we elect to Congress are focused too much on raising money and not enough on creating jobs, protecting a beleaguered middle class, mending the torn social safety net and securing a sensible energy future.

The House voted to repeal healthcare reform after taking millions of dollars in campaign contributions from medical and insurance interests. Tea Party favorite Jim DeMint, along with eighteen colleagues, introduced a Senate bill to repeal the tepid financial reform bill passed last year [2010]. Collectively, the senators backing repeal of those reforms have taken nearly $50 million in campaign contributions from the very Wall Street interests affected by the law, according to data from the Center for Responsive Politics. House Energy and Commerce Committee hearings sound more like Big Oil/King Coal conventions than an enlightened oversight committee puzzling out our nation's energy future.

Along with their efforts to advance or repeal policies, moneyed interests and their front groups like the US Chamber of Commerce, [former president George W. Bush adviser] Karl Rove's Crossroads consortium, and [billionaire businessmen] David and Charles Koch's Americans for Prosperity are pushing for structural changes to our political system to ensure that only the voices of the elite are heard and everyone else is left to fend for him- or herself. Across the country, big money is on the march. From the assaults on the collective bargaining rights of nurses, teachers and other public employees to targeted strikes against state Fair Elections public financing laws to numerous attacks on voting rights, deep-pocket conservatives are aggressively

Sarah Palin speaks at a Super PAC rally. Total Super PAC spending on 2012 elections, as of September 10, 2012, was over $230 million.

seeking to expand their advantage. These forces are also using the courts; in recent arguments before the Supreme Court, they pushed a case designed to limit Arizona's Clean Elections system.

Efforts at Reform

Against this rising tide of big money, several proposals would begin to rebalance our election system. Fair Elections–style public financing, a constitutional amendment to reverse the Supreme Court's *Citizens United* [*v. Federal Election Commission*] decision, disclosure of the funding behind independent political advertising and shareholder approval policies for corporate political expenditures are all necessary, but each faces tough opposition in the current Congress. That's not to say progress isn't possible. On April 6 Senator Dick Durbin and Representatives John Larson, Walter Jones and Chellie Pingree reintroduced the Fair Elections Now Act—with fifty-four co-sponsors, more than ever before.

> ## FAST FACT
>
> The proposed Fair Elections Now Act would limit federal election campaign contributions to one hundred dollars and have qualified candidates run for Congress on a blend of small donations and public funds.

But to succeed, reform efforts—particularly in the *Citizens United* age—must become part of a larger fight that gives voice to what average Americans think: that our system listens too much to money and too little to people.

And that's exactly what's emerging. A dozen environmental groups came together in early February [2011] to coordinate efforts to expose oil and coal companies' political clout. Community-organizing and faith-based groups together with the Service Employees International Union are fighting to hold banks accountable for the foreclosure crisis, hitting them hard on how they've bought off regulators and politicians.

In Wisconsin, right-wing donors like the billionaire Koch brothers thought they'd hit pay dirt, but what was supposed to be an isolated budget debate awakened and united workers and activists perhaps

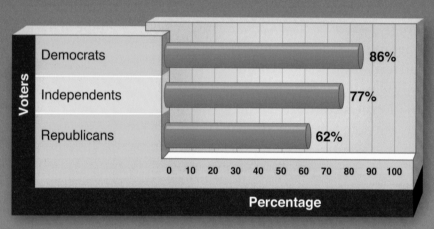

American Voters' Opinion on the Influence of Money in Elections, 2010

This chart shows the percentage of voters in 2010 who wanted immediate action to curb the influence of money in elections.

Voters	Percentage
Democrats	86%
Independents	77%
Republicans	62%

Taken from: Lake Research Partners, "Election Week Polling on Fair Elections Act and Money Campaigns," October 31–November 2, 2010.

more than any event in a generation. Tens of thousands across the country have rallied at statehouses against anti-worker legislation and in solidarity with Wisconsin. On March 16 rank-and-file union members joined reformers and others at a 1,000-person Washington protest against a lobbyist fundraiser for Republican lawmakers from Wisconsin.

A Populist Sentiment

These events add up to a common narrative, one that is rooted in the deeply American belief in government of, by and for the people, not of, by and for the big-money interests. Election-night polling conducted last year [2010] for the Public Campaign Action Fund and Common Cause by Lake Research Partners showed that 75 percent of voters agree that "the amount of money being spent this year on political campaign ads by candidates, political parties, and outside groups poses a real threat to the fairness of our elections and the ability of Congress to get results on our most important issues." Support is strong across party lines, with 62 percent of Republican voters—and 60 percent of Tea Partiers—agreeing that it's urgent for Congress to curb the influence of money in our elections.

When it comes to who controls elections, people at the grassroots don't see big money as blue or red. Americans of every stripe know there's a "buy-partisan" problem. Issue organizations and membership groups—and office seekers across the country—would be strategically wise to seize this populist sentiment and wield it like a club against politicians who defend the cash-and-carry status quo.

To ignore this challenge is to surrender. On so many fights— holding big banks accountable, shifting to a green energy economy, forcing a debate on revenues as part of state budget discussions— there is a critical choice. Will we allow a few well-heeled, unrepresentative special interests to continue to call the shots and let the rest of America foot the bill? Or will we fight back and revitalize the notion of an America for the many, not the money?

EVALUATING THE AUTHOR'S ARGUMENTS:

In this viewpoint Nick Nyhart and David Donnelly claim that the influence of big money in elections is out of control. Using what was written in the previous two viewpoints, what do you think Nyhart and Donnelly would say about the US Supreme Court's decision in *Citizens United v. Federal Election Commission* (2010)?

Efforts to Implement Campaign-Finance Regulations Should End

"The Supreme Court has ruled that campaign-finance restrictions can't be justified on the basis of equality of voice."

John Samples

In the following viewpoint, John Samples argues that attempts at campaign-finance regulations have failed and have rightly been eliminated. Samples contends that efforts to restrict contributions to political campaigns stifle free speech. Furthermore, he claims that there is no evidence that regulations have eliminated corruption, and he contends that money does not have as much influence as people think.

Samples is director of the Center for Representative Government at the Cato Institute and author of *The Fallacy of Campaign Finance Reform.*

AS YOU READ, CONSIDER THE FOLLOWING QUESTIONS:
1. According to the author, in what year were the first major campaign-finance regulations passed?
2. Rather than the influence of money, the author says, political scientists have found what three things that explain lawmaking?
3. Samples claims that it is easier for Americans to blame moneyed interests for America's problems rather than face what democratic failing?

I n 1969, Congress considered the first of the modern era's many campaign-finance regulations. Major laws followed in 1974 and again in 2002. But now that the Supreme Court has invalidated much of the latter as well as some earlier prohibitions on business and union spending, the end of "campaign-finance reform" seems near. Many will lament its passing. Fewer will note its failures.

A Threat to Free Speech

To diminish private political spending, lawmakers can restrict contributions or subsidize candidates. The latter approach, public financing, has never been very popular with voters, so federal law is filled with

The Campaign for Mental Health Reform is one of many so-called Super PACs. The author argues that efforts to restrict political campaign contributions from such organizations limits their free speech.

The Campaign for
Mental Health Reform
Real Crisis... Real People... Real Solutions

limits and prohibitions. Such limits invariably threaten free speech. The early campaign-finance legislation mentioned above would have limited candidates' spending on broadcast advertising, effectively suppressing some political speech. Restrictions on the political spending of corporations and labor unions, meanwhile, were a prior restraint on speech, a particularly severe form of censorship.

Such restrictions have been justified as preventing corruption, as campaign donors might buy official favors. Of course, bribery is already illegal, so corruption is redefined as "undue influence." The trouble is that those who stand to lose or gain much from public policy have every incentive to fight for their interests through political spending. If they succeed, have they had undue influence? Or is that just another way of saying the wrong side won?

Moreover, there is little evidence that money has much influence on policymakers. Political scientists have found that contributions explain little about lawmaking once ideology, party, and constituency are accounted for. One scholarly study of lobbying concluded that "the direct correlation between money and outcomes that so many political scientists have sought simply is not there."

The Failure of Campaign-Finance Restrictions

Reformers also seek equality: If each voter has one vote, why should some be allowed to speak more loudly than others? But the Supreme Court has ruled that campaign-finance restrictions can't be justified on the basis of equality of voice. Making voices equal requires shutting up voices that are speaking "too much." We face a stark choice between equality and freedom of speech, and the Constitution rightly favors the latter.

Even as they fail to deliver benefits, campaign-finance regulations impose costs. The incumbents who write them are tempted to make it harder for challengers to raise money. Scholars have also found that reducing campaign spending leads to fewer and less-informed voters.

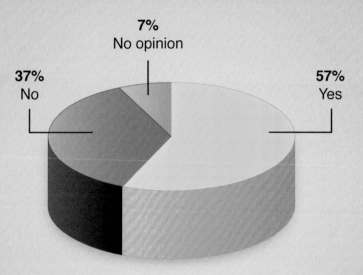

Campaign Money and Free Speech

Should campaign donations be considered a form of free speech?

7%
No opinion

37%
No

57%
Yes

Figures total more than 100 percent, due to rounding.

Taken from: Gallup/First Amendment Center, October 1–2, 2009.

In addition, those engaged in politics seek to legally evade regulations. So reformers constantly demand new regulations to close "loopholes," producing a complex body of law. Legal advice becomes vital for electoral engagement, discouraging participation—a perverse result for rules purporting to advance democracy.

Misplaced Blame

Finally, the rhetoric of campaign-finance reform has poisoned public debate. Instead of arguments, voters hear accusations of corruption. Not surprisingly, many attribute problems to malevolent "moneyed interests."

But our fiscal challenges, for example, come from popular and inadequately funded entitlement programs. No surprise there: Voters' desire for benefits without costs is a very democratic failing. But it is a failing Americans have refused to face; it's easier to blame moneyed interests for our problems.

A day may come when Americans are mature enough to face our collective problems, and campaign spending will no longer be at the center of our discourse. We will debate the merits of policies in a world without demonic money men or divine reformers. And we will have a better politics—a politics freed from the illusions and failings of campaign-finance reform.

EVALUATING THE AUTHOR'S ARGUMENTS:

In this viewpoint John Samples claims that at issue with campaign-finance reform is a choice between equality and freedom of speech. What other controversial social issue can you think of that embodies a conflict between equality and freedom of speech?

Congress Should Pass the DISCLOSE Act

"A vote to oppose [the DISCLOSE Act] is nothing less than a vote to allow corporate and special interest takeovers of our elections."

Barack Obama

In the following viewpoint, President Barack Obama urges the Senate to join the House of Representatives in passing the Democracy Is Strengthened by Casting Light on Spending in Elections (DISCLOSE) Act. Obama claims that the bill is a commonsense reform that simply requires disclosure about who is behind campaign ads. He contends that opposing such a bill will allow dangerous, unlimited corporate spending, without accountability, in the political system.

Obama is the forty-fourth president of the United States.

AS YOU READ, CONSIDER THE FOLLOWING QUESTIONS:
1. According to the author, what US Supreme Court decision allows corporations to spend unlimited amounts of money in elections?
2. Obama charges the Senate Republicans with preventing votes on what other two issues outside of the DISCLOSE Act?
3. What previous president warned of the dangers of limitless corporate spending, according to Obama?

Barack Obama, "Remarks by the President on the DISCLOSE Act," Whitehouse.gov, July 26, 2010.
Courtesy of Whitehouse.gov. All rights reserved. Reproduced by permission.

Because of the Supreme Court's decision earlier this year [2010] in the *Citizens United [v. Federal Election Commission]* case, big corporations—even foreign-controlled ones—are now allowed to spend unlimited amounts of money on American elections. They can buy millions of dollars worth of TV ads—and worst of all, they don't even have to reveal who's actually paying for the ads. Instead, a group can hide behind a name like "Citizens for a Better Future," even if a more accurate name would be "Companies for Weaker Oversight." These shadow groups are already forming and building war chests of tens of millions of dollars to influence the fall elections.

A Commonsense Reform

Now, imagine the power this will give special interests over politicians. Corporate lobbyists will be able to tell members of Congress if they don't vote the right way, they will face an onslaught of negative ads in their next campaign. And all too often, no one will actually know who's really behind those ads.

> ### FAST FACT
>
> Efforts in the US Senate to end filibuster on the DISCLOSE Act by voting to place a time limit on consideration of the act failed to garner the necessary sixty votes, first in July 2010 and again in September 2010.

So the House has already passed a bipartisan bill that would change all this before the next election. The DISCLOSE [Democracy Is Strengthened by Casting Light on Spending in Elections] Act would simply require corporate political advertisers to reveal who's funding their activities. So when special interests take to the airwaves, whoever is running and funding the ad would have to appear in the advertisement and claim responsibility for it—like a company's CEO [chief executive officer] or the organization's biggest contributor. And foreign-controlled corporations and entities would be restricted from spending money to influence American elections—just as they were in the past.

Now, you'd think that making these reforms would be a matter of common sense, particularly since they primarily involve just making

President Barack Obama speaks on campaign financing reform at the White House. Obama thinks the names of financial sponsors of political campaign ads should be made public.

sure that folks who are financing these ads are disclosed so that the American people can make up their own minds. Nobody is saying you can't run the ads—just make sure that people know who in fact is behind financing these ads. And you'd think that reducing corporate and even foreign influence over our elections would not be a partisan

issue. But of course, this is Washington in 2010. And the Republican leadership in the Senate is once again using every tactic and every maneuver they can to prevent the DISCLOSE Act from even coming up for an up or down vote. Just like they did with unemployment insurance for Americans who'd lost their jobs in this recession. Just like they're doing by blocking tax credits and lending assistance for small business owners. On issue after issue, we are trying to move America forward, and they keep on trying to take us back.

At a time of such challenge for America, we can't afford these political games. Millions of Americans are struggling to get by, and their voices shouldn't be drowned out by millions of dollars in secret, special interest advertising. The American people's voices should be heard.

A Danger to Democracy

A vote to oppose these reforms is nothing less than a vote to allow corporate and special interest takeovers of our elections. It is damaging to our democracy. It is precisely what led a Republican President named Theodore Roosevelt to tackle this issue a century ago.

Back then, President Roosevelt warned of the dangers of limitless corporate spending in our political system. He actually called it "one of the principal sources of corruption in our political affairs." And he proposed strict limits on corporate influence in elections not because he was opposed to them expressing their views in the halls of democracy, but he didn't want everybody else being drowned out.

He said, "Every special interest is entitled to justice, but no one is entitled—not one is entitled to a vote in Congress, or a voice on the bench, or to representation in any public office," because he understood those weren't individual voters—these are amalgams of special interests. They have the right to hire their lobbyists. They have the right to put forward their view. They even have the right to advertise. But the least we should be able to do is know who they are.

So we face the sort of challenge that Teddy Roosevelt talked about over a century ago. We've got a similar opportunity to prevent special interests from gaining even more clout in Washington. This should not be a Democratic issue or a Republican issue. This is an issue that goes to whether or not we're going to have a government that works for ordinary Americans; a government of, by and for the people.

That's why these reforms are so important, and that's why I urge the Senate to pass the DISCLOSE Act.

[Editor's note: The Senate failed to advance the DISCLOSE Act in September 2010.]

EVALUATING THE AUTHOR'S ARGUMENTS:

In this viewpoint Barack Obama claims that failure to require disclosure of who is behind campaign ad spending will allow corporate and special-interest takeovers of elections. What assertion about the impact of disclosure is implicit in this reasoning?

Viewpoint
6

Congress Should Not Pass the DISCLOSE Act

Jacob Sullum

"The [DISCLOSE Act's] onerous, lopsided requirements suggest its supporters are more interested in silencing their critics."

In the following viewpoint, Jacob Sullum argues that the proposed Democracy Is Strengthened by Casting Light on Spending in Elections (DISCLOSE) Act would threaten free speech. Sullum claims that the various bans on political speech apply inconsistently to different types of organizations. He also contends that regulations on political speech are onerous and have a chilling effect on what should be legitimate free speech.

Sullum is a senior editor at *Reason* magazine and a nationally syndicated columnist.

AS YOU READ, CONSIDER THE FOLLOWING QUESTIONS:

1. The author refers to what current US Supreme Court justice who criticized campaign-finance laws in 1996?
2. According to Sullum, the DISCLOSE Act would prohibit corporations from engaging in campaign speech if more than what percent of their equity was owned by foreign nationals?
3. Sullum worries that the ad statements required by the DISCLOSE Act would consume approximately what portion of a thirty-second TV ad?

In a 1996 law review article, Supreme Court [justice] Elena Kagan warned that campaign finance laws "easily can serve as incumbent-protection devices, insulating current officeholders from challenge and criticism." The DISCLOSE [Democracy Is Strengthened by Casting Light on Spending in Elections] Act, a speech-squelching bill supported by the man who nominated Kagan [i.e., Barack Obama], is a good example.

The DISCLOSE Act

President Obama and congressional Democrats say the DISCLOSE Act, which is expected to come up for a vote soon, is aimed at ensuring transparency and preventing corruption in the wake of *Citizens United v. FEC* [*Federal Election Commission*], the January [2010] decision in which the Supreme Court lifted restrictions on political speech by

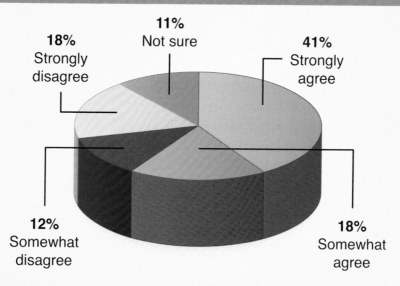

Survey on the Prohibition of Political Ads

Percentage of people who believe that a law prohibiting businesses that have been awarded government contracts from running political ads should also apply to unions representing workers employed by government contractors:

18% Strongly disagree

11% Not sure

41% Strongly agree

12% Somewhat disagree

18% Somewhat agree

Taken from: Pulse Opinion Research Survey, September 12, 2010.

corporations and unions. But the bill's onerous, lopsided requirements suggest its supporters are more interested in silencing their critics.

Consider the ban on independent expenditures by government contractors, under which thousands of businesses would be forbidden to run ads mentioning a candidate for federal office from 90 days before the primary through the general election. Although this provision is supposed to prevent the exchange of helpful ads for taxpayer money, it applies even to businesses that win contracts through competitive bidding. Furthermore, the ban does not apply to Democrat-friendly, taxpayer-dependent interests such as public employee unions and recipients of government grants.

Likewise, the DISCLOSE Act prohibits corporations from engaging in pre-election political speech if 20 percent or more of their equity is owned by foreign nationals. That provision would bar U.S.-based companies with foreign investors, such as Verizon and ConocoPhillips, from publicly addressing issues that affect their American shareholders and employees. Although the official aim is preventing foreign interference with U.S. elections, the ban would not apply to international unions such as the SEIU [Service Employees International Union] and the UFCW [United Food and Commercial Workers Union] or to international activist groups such as Greenpeace and Human Rights First.

Intimidating and Burdensome Restrictions

Even when corporations are allowed to speak, any communication that mentions a candidate during the covered period, including online material, could expose them to investigation by the Federal Election Commission (FEC) for unauthorized "coordination" with a political campaign. Despite all the rhetoric about big corporations drowning out the voices of ordinary citizens, the prospect of such an inquiry is most likely to intimidate small businesses and grassroots organizations with limited resources and legal expertise.

The DISCLOSE Act would make public the names of sponsors of political advertisements, like this ad for Texas Governor Rick Perry. Opponents of the DISCLOSE Act say that publicizing the sponsors of political campaign ads threatens free speech.

The "stand by your ad" statements required by the DISCLOSE Act also impose a substantial burden on the exercise of First Amendment rights. Under current law, a political ad has to include a statement indicating the sponsoring organization—say, the U.S. Chamber of Commerce or the American Civil Liberties Union. Under the DISCLOSE Act, both the organization's head and its "significant funder" would have to appear in the ad and take responsibility for it. According to the Center for Competitive Politics, these statements would consume one-third to one-half of the time in a 30-second TV spot.

The DISCLOSE Act's reporting requirements are likewise redundant, burdensome, and intimidating. Among other things, an organization's donors are presumed to support its political ads unless they specify otherwise, so their names must be reported to the government, raising the possibility of bullying or retaliation by politicians.

A Chilling Effect on Speech

The anxiety and uncertainty created by the new rules would be compounded by the fact that they would take effect 30 days after the law is enacted, before the FEC would have time to issue regulations clarifying them. Opposing an amendment that would have postponed the effective date until January 1, Rep. Michael Capuano (D-Mass.) said he wants people to worry about a fine or prison sentence when they dare to speak ill of him.

"I hope it chills out all—not one side, all sides!" said Capuano. "I have no problem whatsoever keeping everybody out. If I could keep all outside entities out, I would."

Similarly, Sen. Charles Schumer (D-N.Y.), upon unveiling the bill, said "the deterrent effect should not be underestimated." For those who view nonpoliticians as meddlesome "outside entities" and criticism of incumbents as a crime to be deterred, the chilling effect of campaign finance laws is a feature, not a bug.

EVALUATING THE AUTHOR'S ARGUMENTS:

In this viewpoint Jacob Sullum raises concerns that the "stand by your ad" statements required by the DICSLOSURE Act place a significant burden on the exercise of First Amendment rights. How might Barack Obama, author of the preceding viewpoint, object to his concern?

Chapter 3

How Can the Election Process Be Improved?

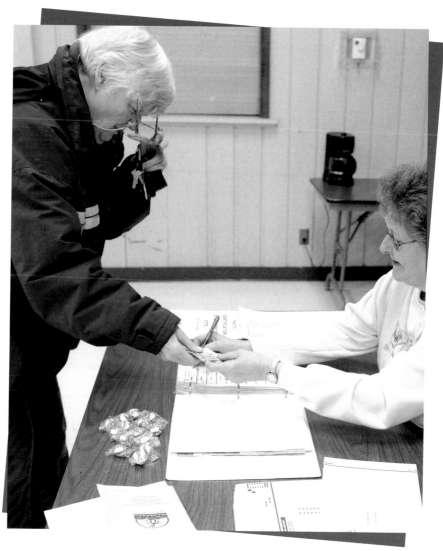

A voter shows her identification to an election official before voting. Whether requiring voter IDs will improve the US election process is hotly debated.

Viewpoint

1

Voters Should Be Required to Show Valid Identification

"Without voter ID, election officials have no way to prevent unscrupulous individuals from casting fraudulent ballots."

Hans A. von Spakovsky

In the following viewpoint, Hans A. von Spakovsky argues that voter identification laws are needed to help prevent fraud at the polls and to ensure confidence in the integrity of elections. Von Spakovsky claims that despite what some critics say, voter ID requirements do not suppress voter turnout, and he gives examples of states with voter ID laws that experienced increased turnout in the last few elections even after implementing such laws.

Von Spakovsky is a senior legal fellow and manager of the Civil Justice Reform Initiative in the Center for Legal and Judicial Studies at the Heritage Foundation, a conservative Washington, DC, think tank.

AS YOU READ, CONSIDER THE FOLLOWING QUESTIONS:

1. According to the author, which six states recently passed voter ID laws?
2. What two states does von Spakovsky mention as showing increased voter turnout following passage of voter ID laws?
3. Von Spakovsky claims that opponents of voter ID laws have filed lawsuits with the claim that the laws result in what?

Laws requiring voters to present valid identification before casting their ballots are growing in popularity. Six states—Georgia, Indiana, Texas, Rhode Island, South Carolina and Kansas—have recently passed voter ID laws, and more have them under consideration.

Opponents of these laws have raised absurd objections, equating passage with the reimposition of Jim Crow [laws whose hidden intent was to continue racial segregation] and asserting that the real motive is to suppress voter turnout. Such rancorous attacks defy common sense and the views of the American people. Requiring voters to authenticate their identity is necessary to ensure the integrity and security of our election process.

Voter ID can help prevent impersonation fraud at the polls, voting under fictitious voter registrations, double voting by individuals registered in more than one state and voting by illegal aliens. As the U.S. Supreme Court recognized when it upheld Indiana's voter ID law in 2008, "flagrant examples of such fraud have been documented throughout this Nation's history by respected historians and journalists."

A woman applies for a driver's license so she will have a photo ID to comply with new voter ID laws in Tennessee. Proponents say this is the only way to prevent voter fraud.

That opinion was written by Supreme Court Justice John Paul Stevens. Though one of the most liberal members of the Supreme Court, Justice Stevens had practiced law in Chicago [where voter fraud was often rampant] before serving on the court. Small wonder he found the claim that voter fraud does not exist to be absurd.

States pass voter ID laws not just to deter and detect voter fraud, but also so that their citizens can be confident in the integrity of their elections. Despite what critics like [civil rights leader] Jesse Jackson say, voter ID is supported by the vast majority of the American people—and that support crosses all ethnic, racial and party lines. It is not "Jim Crow" and it is not "voter suppression."

Numerous studies have shown that requiring an ID to vote does not depress turnout. Georgia and Indiana have had several elections since they implemented voter ID laws. Turnout has gone up in those states, including the turnout of minority voters. In fact, turnout in the 2008 presidential election (the first election held after their photo ID laws went into effect) increased more dramatically in Georgia and Indiana than [it] did in some states without photo ID.

Black voter turnout increased in Georgia not only in the presidential election (compared to the 2004 race when there was no photo ID law), but also in the 2010 midterm election (compared to the previous midterm). As Georgia's Secretary of State noted recently, turnout in the 2010 election "among African Americans outpaced the growth of that population's pool of registered voters by more than 20 percentage points."

Indiana experienced similar results. In the 2008 election, turnout among Democrats increased by 8.32 percentage points from 2004 when there was no voter ID law. It was the largest increase in Democratic turnout of any state in the nation. In 2010, Indiana had a "large and impressive" increase in black turnout. According to the Joint Center for Political and Economic Studies, "the black share of

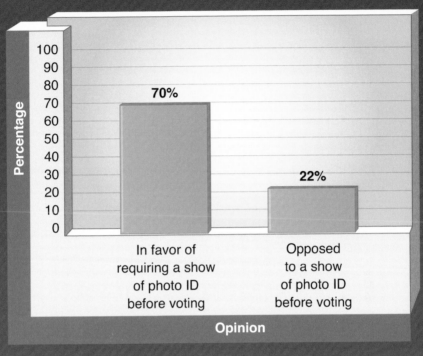

Taken from: Rasmussen Reports Survey, December 18–19, 2011. www.rasmussenreports.com.

the state vote was higher in 2010 than it was in 2008, a banner year for black turnout."

Opponents raised the specious "mass disfranchisement" claim in lawsuits filed against the Georgia and Indiana laws. The courts threw out the claims. As an Indiana federal district court observed, "despite apocalyptic assertions of wholesale voter disenfranchisement, Plaintiffs have produced not a single piece of evidence of any identifiable registered voter who would be prevented from voting." The NAACP [National Association for the Advancement of Colored People], a plaintiff in the Georgia case, could not find a single member who would be unable to vote because of the ID requirement.

As the Supreme Court correctly observed, fraud can change the outcome of close elections. Without voter ID, election officials have no way to prevent unscrupulous individuals from casting fraudulent ballots. For those trying to defend America's electoral integrity, the stakes are high. We have an obligation and a duty to secure our elections so that voters can choose their representatives. To do otherwise, is to risk the future of our republic.

EVALUATING THE AUTHOR'S ARGUMENTS:

In this viewpoint Hans A. von Spakovsky cites evidence of increased voter turnout in states that implemented voter ID laws to support his claim that the laws do not suppress turnout. Do you think the fact that the national turnout for the 2008 presidential election was the highest in years affects the author's argument? Why or why not?

Viewpoint
2

Misidentified Priorities

Tova Wang

> "The truth
> is that many
> legislators
> are trying to
> enact voter-
> ID laws . . .
> so that they
> can control
> who votes."

In the following viewpoint, Tova Wang argues that voter identification laws are unnecessary, expensive, and an attempt to discourage voting among certain populations. Wang claims that although the justification for voter ID laws is to prevent fraud, there is little evidence for the type of fraud prevented by identification. She claims that voter ID laws unfairly target people who do not have identification, and she also claims that ID laws that provide for free identification are a misuse of resources.

Wang is senior democracy fellow at Demos and a democracy fellow at the Century Foundation, both progressive think tanks.

AS YOU READ, CONSIDER THE FOLLOWING QUESTIONS:

1. What four states does the author identify as having new Republican leadership in 2011 who are pushing voter ID laws?
2. According to Wang, a study showed that how many people were convicted of or pled guilty to illegal voting from 2002 to 2005?
3. Missouri's Committee on Legislative Research found that implementing a photo-ID law would cost Missouri how much over the first three years, according to Wang?

state Rep. Debbie Riddle, a Republican, camped out in the lobby of Texas' House of Representatives for two days in early November to make sure she was first in line to prefile a bill for the new session.

"I felt it was important to be first to file because I want my bills to have the lowest possible bill numbers," Riddle told *Houston Community Newspapers.* "That doesn't necessarily mean that they are going to pass, but it helps them get into and out of committee quickly."

"The low bill number also shows that I have fire in my belly and that I am serious about getting these bills passed," she added.

What could be so urgent? Had she come up with a way to keep more teachers in the classroom? Create jobs for unemployed Texans wracked by the recession?

No, her bill was for a voter-identification law that would require all voters to produce a photo ID—or two nonphoto IDs—in order to cast a ballot

Riddle is not alone in prioritizing voter-ID laws. With Republicans taking control of state legislatures and governorships cross the country this month, newly emboldened GOP lawmakers in places like North Carolina, Minnesota, Wisconsin, and Kansas are pushing laws that would require photo identification for all voters. Voter-ID bills have already been prefiled—that is, submitted before sessions begin—in at least six states. In North Carolina, legislators have even vowed to pass such a measure in the first hundred days of the session, and incoming Wisconsin Senate Majority Leader Scott Fitzgerald has said a voter-ID law will be the first bill introduced in the 2011 legislative session.

But despite Republican alarmism over rigged elections, voter-ID laws are a solution in search of a problem: They address an exceedingly rare type of vote fraud, cost the state money that could be used to address more pressing issues in a time of economic crisis, and serve primarily to disenfranchise hundreds of thousands of voters—just so politicians can influence who votes in the next election.

Given the sense of urgency behind these laws, one would expect that on Election Day, droves of people scheme to fix elections by impersonating other voters. That's not the case. The type of fraud that voter-identification laws would address—that is, impersonation of another voter at the polling place—is exceedingly rare. An extensive analysis by professor Lori Minnite at Barnard College showed that at the federal level, only 24 people were convicted of or pleaded guilty to illegal voting between 2002 and 2005, an average of eight people a year.

The available state-level evidence of voter fraud, which Minnite culled from interviews, newspapers, and court proceedings, was also negligible. It included 19 people who were ineligible to vote—five because they were still under state supervision for felony convictions and 14 who were not U.S. citizens—and five people who voted twice in the same election. Even an intensive five-year investigation by the Department of Justice under George W. Bush famously netted only 86 voter-fraud convictions. Most of these were for offenses like vote-buying schemes or ineligible voters registering to vote—*not for voter fraud that could have been prevented by a voter-ID law.*

> **FAST FACT**
>
> Three state legislatures—Kansas, Rhode Island, and Wisconsin—enacted new voter identification laws in 2011, whereas three states—Minnesota, New Hampshire, and North Carolina—had proposed ID laws vetoed by their governors.

Voter-ID laws do, however, serve to disenfranchise many voters—primarily people of color, young people, senior citizens, and people with disabilities. Among Americans over the age of 65, 18 percent do not have a photo ID. Fully a quarter of African Americans and 15 percent of low-income voters also don't carry ID. For members of these groups, who tend to have low voter-registration levels anyway, getting an ID becomes just another hurdle to voting—in some cases the virtually insurmountable one of paying what amounts to a poll tax.

One of the great ironies of this latest assault on voting rights is that scarce financial resources are being squandered at a time when states face *real* and serious problems. According to the National Conference on State Legislatures, 35 states and Puerto Rico project

budget gaps for 2012, and a majority of those gaps are greater than or equal to 10 percent of the overall budget. But newly elected Republican legislators have the wind behind them; the Supreme Court's 2008 decision in *Crawford v. Marion County* upheld a voter-ID law in Indiana but required states to provide IDs to those who could not afford them. By the time a state has provided free identification for anyone who needs it, educated voters, and trained poll workers on the new requirement, a voter-ID program will have cost millions of dollars, much of that a recurring expense each year. For example, Missouri's Committee on Legislative Research found that implementing a photo-ID law would cost Missouri close to $6 million in the first year and around $4 million in its second and third years.

Instead of spending money on a nonexistent problem, states could save crucial programs in health care, job creation, and education. They could even use this money to increase voter participation by improving poll-worker recruitment and training, stepping up outreach efforts to Americans whose primary language is not English, and educating citizens about the registration and voting process.

The truth is that many legislators are trying to enact voter-ID laws, which disproportionately discourage voting among populations that tend to support Democrats, so that they can control who votes. Is it a coincidence that after African Americans, Hispanics, and young people voted in historic numbers in 2008 in places like North Carolina that these states are now trying to make it harder for these very groups to vote? Proponents of voter-ID laws don't care about solving crisis-level problems but rather, want to look out for their own interests. When legislative sessions begin this month, the efforts to enact ID laws will likely spread given that Republicans now control 20 state legislatures. Even as states cut major social programs and citizens struggle with the recession, these lawmakers will continue to shape the electorate to their political favor. At least that way, they can save one job in their state—their own.

A National Popular Vote Should Replace the Winner-Take-All Electoral System

Saul Anuzis and Rhett Ruggerio

"National Popular Vote will insure that every state is a battleground and force national candidates to run truly national campaigns."

In the following viewpoint, Saul Anuzis and Rhett Ruggerio argue that the presidential election system should be reformed to eliminate the state-by-state, winner-take-all electoral system and replace it with a nationwide electoral system that reflects the popular vote. The authors claim that this so-called National Popular Vote system would ensure that the candidate with the most popular votes wins and would thus ensure that voters from every state matter.

Anuzis is a former chair for the Michigan Republican Party, and Ruggerio is a former national delegate from the Delaware Democratic Party.

Saul Anuzis and Rhett Ruggerio, "Making Presidential Campaigns National," *Campaigns & Elections,* June 2010. CampaignsAndElections.com. Copyright © 2010 by Campaigns & Elections. All rights reserved. Reproduced by permission.

AS YOU READ, CONSIDER THE FOLLOWING QUESTIONS:

1. According to the authors, 98 percent of the resources of presidential candidates are spent in only how many states?
2. In how many of the nation's presidential elections has a candidate won without winning the most popular votes nationwide, according to Anuzis and Ruggerio?
3. The authors claim that what percentage of Americans support a national popular vote for president?

A s Americans look forward to the next presidential election [in 2012], the political reality of the race will be that the voters in at least 35 states will not matter. As in previous presidential elections, candidates will spend two thirds of their time and money in just six closely divided battleground states. Ninety-eight percent of their resources will be spent in only 15 states.

The National Popular Vote Alternative

That is not what the Founding Fathers envisioned when they carefully crafted the Constitution, which gives exclusive and plenary [full] control to the states over the manner of awarding their electoral votes.

As members of the Republican National Committee and Democratic National Committee, we see another way—one which would create a system where the states keep their plenary authority but where every American citizen's vote matters: A National popular vote.

The National Popular Vote does not abolish the Electoral College. Instead, it uses the states' existing authority to change how the Electoral College is chosen, namely from the current state-by-state count to the popular vote of the people across all 50 states.

FAST FACT

A 2011 Gallup Poll found that 62 percent of Americans would be willing to amend the US Constitution to elect the president by popular vote rather than keep the current system.

This would guarantee the presidency to the candidate who receives the most total popular votes in all 50 states.

The Problem with the Current System

The shortcomings of the current system stem from the winner-take-all rule (i.e., awarding all of a state's electoral votes to the candidate who receives the most popular votes in each state).

Because of the winner-take-all rule, a candidate can win the presidency without winning the most popular votes nationwide. This has occurred in four of the nation's 56 presidential elections. The 2004 election could have been the fifth: A shift of fewer than 60,000 votes in Ohio would have defeated President [George W.] Bush despite his nationwide lead of 3,500,000 votes.

While the Constitution gives the states exclusive and plenary control, it does not establish or anticipate a winner-take-all system. It was not the Founders' choice and was used by only three states in the nation's first presidential election in 1789. Maine and Nebraska currently award electoral votes by congressional district—a reminder that

New Jersey's fifteen presidential electors are sworn in. Many Americans want the electoral college system replaced by a national popular vote system.

Impact of the Current Electoral College Rules

Following the 2008 presidential conventions, Ohio, a swing state, received more postconvention campaign visits and more campaign spending than the twenty-five smallest states combined.

Share of Population, 2008 Estimates

Share of Postconvention, Campaign Visits, 2008

Share of Postconvention, Campaign Spending, 2008

Taken from: FairVote.org, September 2011.

state action is the constitutionally appropriate approach to determine the way the president is elected.

Under the National Popular Vote, all the electoral votes from the enacting states would be awarded to the presidential candidate who receives the most popular votes in all 50 states. The bill would take effect only when enacted by states possessing a majority of the electoral votes—that is, enough electoral votes to elect a president (270 of 538). The bill would replace the current state-by-state system of awarding electoral votes with a system that represents the will of the people from across the country.

The Popularity of Reform

As of today, the National Popular Vote Bill has been passed by 29 legislative chambers in 19 states. A 2007 poll showed 72 percent support nationwide for a national popular vote for the president. This reform of our presidential election system would guarantee that every vote matters, that every state is relevant and that every town and community would have the same value to each and every candidate for president in every presidential election. It would make a vote in Grand Rapids, Michigan or Dover, Delaware as important to the outcome as votes in Sarasota, Florida and Dayton, Ohio.

National Popular Vote will insure that every state is a battleground and force national candidates to run truly national campaigns. We believe this will have the net result of strengthening state parties, as they will be critical in turning out voters in all 50 states.

Currently, the Senate chambers of our home states of Michigan and Delaware are considering a state-based plan for electing the president by national popular vote. The same bill passed the Michigan and Delaware Houses of Representatives with strong bipartisan support.

Yet just as importantly, from our perspective, the National Popular Vote bill would guarantee the presidency to the candidate who receives the most popular votes in all 50 states and would truly nationalize a candidate's legitimacy and mandate.

EVALUATING THE AUTHOR'S ARGUMENTS:

In this viewpoint Saul Anuzis and Rhett Ruggerio claim that the Founding Fathers did not envision the current electoral system. In what way does Sean Parnell, author of the following viewpoint, disagree?

> "The Electoral College ensures that in order to be elected President, a candidate must appeal to not only a majority or even [a] plurality of voters, but also to voters from a geographical cross-section of the country."

A National Popular Vote Should Not Replace the Current Electoral System

Sean Parnell

In the following viewpoint, Sean Parnell argues that the current Electoral College system should not be replaced by the National Popular Vote (NPV) proposal. Parnell claims that the current method is a check on majority rule and ensures that there is a strong link between a state's citizens and its electoral votes. He also raises concerns that the NPV plan is too fragile and will not result in presidential candidates addressing the concerns of more voters.

Parnell is president of Impact Policy Management, a public policy firm, and the former president of the Center for Competitive Politics.

1. According to the author, approximately how old is the current Electoral College system?
2. What situation does Parnell give as possibly tempting a state legislature to abandon a compact to use the National Popular Vote?
3. The author claims that under the National Popular Vote system, candidates are likely to spend most of their time campaigning to what demographic?

The National Popular Vote (NPV) proposal would represent a fundamental shift in how our nation elects the President. While many well-intentioned individuals and organizations support this cause and compelling arguments can be made in its favor, the NPV plan ultimately represents a scheme that creates more problems than it purports to solve and would largely fail to achieve the outcomes desired by its proponents.

The Center for Competitive Politics has prepared this memo to briefly review and summarize some of the key shortcomings of the NPV compact as well as to provide a listing of more extensive research and analysis on this subject.

A Check on Majority Rule

The NPV plan would jettison a nearly 220-year-old system for electing our nation's President. In doing so, it would reject one of the many carefully-crafted checks on majority rule designed by the Founding Fathers to safeguard minority rights.

The Electoral College ensures that in order to be elected President, a candidate must appeal to not only a majority or even [a] plurality of voters, but also to voters from a geographical cross-section of the country. This system requires that candidates for the highest office in the land are not able to simply rely on highly energized, sympathetic, and homogeneous voters concentrated in only a few densely-populated parts of the country.

Instead, candidates must be able to appeal to multiple constituencies, building broad coalitions based on policies that address the needs

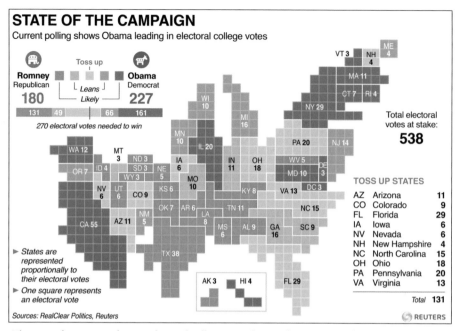

STATE OF THE CAMPAIGN

Current polling shows Obama leading in electoral college votes

Romney Republican **180**

Toss up

Obama Democrat **227**

| 131 | 49 | | 66 | 161 |

270 electoral votes needed to win

Total electoral votes at stake: **538**

TOSS UP STATES

AZ	Arizona	11
CO	Colorado	9
FL	Florida	29
IA	Iowa	6
NV	Nevada	6
NH	New Hampshire	4
NC	North Carolina	15
OH	Ohio	18
PA	Pennsylvania	20
VA	Virginia	13
	Total	**131**

▶ States are represented proportionally to their electoral votes

▶ One square represents an electoral vote

Sources: RealClear Politics, Reuters

REUTERS

This map shows an update on electoral college votes during the 2012 presidential race. The electoral college system has worked for 220 years, so those who favor it see no reason to replace it. (© Reuters/Landov)

and interests of Americans across the country. The [NPV] plan would eliminate the need for candidates to build these coalitions in support of their candidacies, allowing them instead to focus on issues that appeal to and motivate their partisan base.

The requirement that candidates appeal to voters across the country and not just in a handful of populous areas is an important check on the power of a narrowly-focused majority to trample the rights of the minority. The NPV scheme would eliminate this important check.

The States' Interests

Another important deficiency with the plan is that it severs the intrinsic link between a state's citizens and a state's electoral votes. Instead of each state's electoral votes being determined based on the interests of its citizens, a state's electoral votes are allocated based on criteria having little, if anything, to do with the interests and preferences of its citizens.

Advocates of the NPV plan claim that states have not always relied on citizens' votes to allocate their electoral votes. For example, early in American history several states gave the power to appoint electors directly to the state legislature.

However, even then, the electors were appointed by officials that were accountable to the state's voters, and presumably were required to heed the interests and preferences of their citizens. The NPV compact breaks this vital connection, allowing for a state's electoral votes to be awarded based on criteria wholly unrelated to the interests and preferences of the state's citizens.

For example, if the state legislature can award electoral votes based on election results outside of its jurisdiction, could the legislature also simply delegate the power to appoint electors to a special commission? Could they establish a system of choosing electors that sought to "correct" or "balance out" perceived inequities in the demographics of who votes and who does not? Could they substitute for the recorded totals of nationwide votes an estimate based on how the vote would have turned out if only other states had run "fair" elections?

By cutting the link between a state's voters and a state's electoral votes, the NPV plan would open a Pandora's Box of possibilities for alternate methods of awarding electoral votes.

A Fragile Compact

Abandoning the Electoral College as it presently operates would also create significant opportunities for political gamesmanship as states may seek to obtain partisan advantage for one party or another by entering or leaving the compact (or threatening to do so), if it seems advantageous at any given moment.

For example, a state legislature may conclude late in the election cycle that a candidate overwhelmingly favored by its voters is unlikely to win a majority or plurality nationwide, but might win the Presidency if the state were to revert to the traditional Electoral College. As state legislators are only accountable to their own voters, and not any sort of national majority, they may conclude it is in their best interest to abandon the NPV plan.

Taken from: US Election Assistance Commission, "The Electoral College," January 2011. www.eac.gov.

The temptation to withdraw from the compact under such a scenario would be irresistible to some. One need only recall the partisan maneuvering regarding a Massachusetts U.S. Senate seat in 2004, when a legislature controlled by Democrats stripped a Republican governor of the power to appoint a replacement in the event that John Kerry won the presidency, and again in 2009 when the Democratic legislature restored the power to appoint a replacement to a Democratic governor when it appeared doing so would provide the U.S. Senate with a timely 60th vote for health care reform.

Because the authority to determine how a state's electors are appointed is given exclusively to the state legislature, it may well be that a state cannot delegate that power to a body not under its jurisdiction, i.e. the other 49 states. It is thus uncertain whether a state could legally withdraw from the compact even though NPV supporters claim that states cannot. Nevertheless, simply the attempt to do so would spur nationwide outrage and chaos, leading to court battles reminiscent of *Bush v. Gore* in the 2000 election. . . .

A Change in Campaigning

Finally, the belief of NPV advocates that abandoning the Electoral College will ensure candidates reach out to and address the concerns of more voters is simply not accurate.

All elections require candidates to make strategic decisions about which voters to reach out to, in what manner, and how often. Because resources are scarce, especially candidates' time, a presidential campaign under the NPV system would simply require candidates to allocate their scarce resources differently, perhaps choosing to ignore different voters than they do now but inevitably choosing to devote few if any resources to broad swaths of the public.

In fact, the NPV plan is likely to increase candidates' time spent on addressing the needs and issues of "base" voters while decreasing outreach to undecided and independent voters. Rather than appealing to a broad cross-section of voters in different states around the country, it would be in a candidate's self-interest to appeal primarily to well-organized constituencies with large and motivated national memberships.

Candidates are also likely to spend more time in urban and suburban areas, where potential votes are far more plentiful. Whereas, under the current system, doing a Presidential campaign event in smaller, rural communities might make sense in order to garner enough votes to win a specific state's electoral votes, under the NPV system, there is little reason for candidates to venture outside of densely-populated areas.

EVALUATING THE AUTHOR'S ARGUMENTS:

In this viewpoint Sean Parnell says that the current Electoral College system ensures that a presidential candidate must appeal to voters from diverse geographical locations. From your knowledge of the Electoral College taken from the viewpoints, elaborate on how he might believe the system does this.

There Are Good Reasons in Favor of Mandatory Voting

William A. Galston

"Jury duty is mandatory; why not voting?"

In the following viewpoint, William A. Galston argues that America should try making voting mandatory. Galston claims that compulsory voting reinforces civic duty, increases democracy, and could remedy political polarization. He points to the implementation of mandatory voting in Australia in support of his view that the practice could work in the United States.

Galston is the Ezra K. Zilkha Chair in Governance Studies and a senior fellow at the Brookings Institution and the Saul I. Stern Professor of Civic Engagement at the University of Maryland.

AS YOU READ, CONSIDER THE FOLLOWING QUESTIONS:

1. According to Galston, in what year did Australia adopt mandatory voting?
2. The author claims that because of differences in the US political system, voter turnout rates were much higher in which two decades?
3. According to the author, approximately what fraction of US voters turns out for presidential elections?

Jury duty is mandatory; why not voting? The idea seems vaguely un-American. Maybe so, but it's neither unusual nor undemocratic. And it would ease the intense partisan polarization that weakens our capacity for self-government and public trust in our governing institutions.

Mandatory Voting Around the World

Thirty-one countries have some form of mandatory voting, according to the International Institute for Democracy and Electoral Assistance. The list includes nine members of the Organization for Economic Cooperation and Development and two-thirds of the Latin American nations. More than half back up the legal requirement with an enforcement mechanism, while the rest are content to rely on the moral force of the law.

Despite the prevalence of mandatory voting in so many democracies, it's easy to dismiss the practice as a form of statism that couldn't work in America's individualistic and libertarian political culture. But consider Australia, whose political culture is closer to that of the United States than that of any other English-speaking country. Alarmed by a decline in voter turnout to less than 60 percent in 1922, Australia adopted mandatory voting in 1924, backed by small fines (roughly the size of traffic tickets) for nonvoting, rising with repeated acts of nonparticipation. The law established permissible reasons for not voting, like illness and foreign travel, and allows citizens who faced fines for not voting to defend themselves.

The results were remarkable. In the 1925 election, the first held under the new law, turnout soared to 91 percent. In recent elections, it has hovered around 95 percent. The law also changed civic norms. Australians are more likely than before to see voting as an obligation. The negative side effects many feared did not materialize. For example, the percentage of ballots intentionally spoiled or completed randomly as acts of resistance remained on the order of 2 to 3 percent.

A Support for Democracy

Proponents offer three reasons in favor of mandatory voting. The first is straightforwardly civic. A democracy can't be strong if its citizenship is weak. And right now American citizenship is

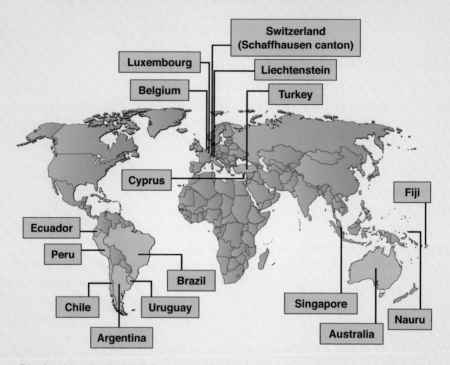

A Sampling of Countries with Enforced Compulsory Voting

Switzerland (Schaffhausen canton)

Luxembourg

Liechtenstein

Belgium

Turkey

Cyprus

Fiji

Ecuador

Peru

Brazil

Chile

Uruguay

Singapore

Nauru

Argentina

Australia

Taken from: International Institute for Democracy and Electoral Assistance, "Compulsory Voting," updated March 2009. www.iddea.int.

attenuated—strong on rights, weak on responsibilities. There is less and less that being a citizen requires of us, especially after the abolition of the draft. Requiring people to vote in national elections once every two years would reinforce the principle of reciprocity at the heart of citizenship.

The second argument for mandatory voting is democratic. Ideally, a democracy will take into account the interests and views of all citizens. But if some regularly vote while others don't, officials are likely to give greater weight to participants. This might not matter much if nonparticipants were evenly distributed through the population. But political scientists have long known that they aren't. People with lower levels of income and education are less likely to vote, as are young adults and recent first-generation immigrants.

Changes in our political system have magnified these disparities. During the 1950s and '60s, when turnout rates were much higher, political parties reached out to citizens year-round. At the local level these parties, which reformers often criticized as "machines," connected even citizens of modest means and limited education with neighborhood institutions and gave them a sense of participation in national politics as well. (In its heyday, organized labor reinforced these effects.) But in the absence of these more organic forms of political mobilization, the second-best option is a top-down mechanism of universal mobilization.

Mandatory voting would tend to even out disparities stemming from income, education and age, enhancing our system's inclusiveness. It is true, as some object, that an enforcement mechanism would impose greater burdens on those with fewer resources. But this makes it all the more likely that these citizens would respond by going to the polls, and they would stand to gain far more than the cost of a traffic ticket.

FAST FACT

In the 2008 presidential election, 65 percent of eligible voters voted, whereas just over 40 percent voted in the 2010 midterm election.

A Remedy for Polarization

The third argument for mandatory voting goes to the heart of our current ills. Our low turnout rate pushes American politics toward increased polarization. The reason is that hard-core partisans are more likely to dominate lower-turnout elections, while those who are less fervent about specific issues and less attached to political organizations tend not to participate at levels proportional to their share of the electorate.

A distinctive feature of our constitutional system—elections that are quadrennial for president but biennial for the House of Representatives—magnifies these effects. It's bad enough that only three-fifths of the electorate turns out to determine the next president, but much worse that only two-fifths of our citizens vote in House elections two years later. If events combine to energize one part of the political spectrum and dishearten the other, a relatively small portion of the electorate can shift the system out of all proportion to its numbers.

Voters go to the polls in Australia where voting is mandatory, and 95 percent of voters cast their ballots.

Some observers are comfortable with this asymmetry. But if you think that today's intensely polarized politics impedes governance and exacerbates mistrust—and that is what most Americans firmly (and in my view rightly) believe—then you should be willing to consider reforms that would strengthen the forces of conciliation.

A Worthy Experiment

Imagine our politics with laws and civic norms that yield near-universal voting. Campaigns could devote far less money to costly, labor-intensive get-out-the-vote efforts. Media gurus wouldn't have the same incentive to drive down turnout with negative advertising. Candidates would know that they must do more than mobilize their bases with red-meat rhetoric on hot-button issues. Such a system would improve not only electoral politics but also the legislative process. Rather than focusing on symbolic gestures whose major purpose is to agitate partisans, Congress might actually roll up its sleeves and tackle the serious, complex issues it ignores.

The United States is not Australia, of course, and there's no guarantee that the similarity of our political cultures would produce equivalent political results. For example, reforms of general elections would leave untouched the distortions generated by party primaries in which small numbers of voters can shape the choices for the entire electorate. And the United States Constitution gives the states enormous power over voting procedures. Mandating voting nationwide would go counter to our traditions (and perhaps our Constitution) and would encounter strong state opposition. Instead, a half-dozen states from parts of the country with different civic traditions should experiment with the practice, and observers—journalists, social scientists, citizens' groups and elected officials—would monitor the consequences.

We don't know what the outcome would be. But one thing is clear: If we do nothing and allow a politics of passion to define the bounds of the electorate, as it has for much of the last four decades, the prospect for a less polarized, more effective political system that enjoys the trust and confidence of the people is not bright.

EVALUATING THE AUTHOR'S ARGUMENTS:

In this viewpoint William A. Galston does not make use of quotations. How might quotations from Australians, who have a mandatory voting system, improve Galston's argument?

"Opinions may differ on whether greater voter turnout is a good thing, but no one should support policies designed to force people to be free."

There Are Good Reasons to Oppose Mandatory Voting

Fred L. Smith

In the following viewpoint, Fred L. Smith argues that mandatory voting involves the contradictory use of force to encourage freedom. Smith claims that forcing uninformed voters to the polls is not good for society, and he contends there is no reason to think it will decrease political polarization. Furthermore, Smith denies that voting is analogous to jury duty, claiming that the former is a right whereas the latter is a duty.

Smith is president and founder of the Competitive Enterprise Institute, a free-market public policy group.

AS YOU READ, CONSIDER THE FOLLOWING QUESTIONS:

1. Smith claims that in any given election, over what percentage of eligible voters will not go to the polls?
2. What does the author say about Australia in support of his view that compulsory voting will not eliminate polarization?
3. According to Smith, no fewer than how many amendments to the US Constitution mention the right to vote?

Government should not force people to be free.

Big government "solutions" for every social problem under the sun are all around us. I thought I'd seen them all—until recently, when I found myself debating a statist proposal to *cure apathy.* Norman Ornstein of the American Enterprise Institute and I recently debated mandatory voting. He argued in favor and I in opposition. Ornstein brought up many interesting points, however, and I feel compelled to present my thorough responses below. I have always held the expansion of liberty as the most important goal of public policy, but it cannot be achieved through forceful regulation. The use of force to encourage freedom, I believe, is self-contradictory and practically and morally wrong.

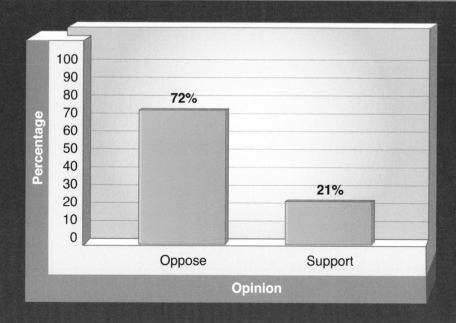

Americans Oppose Compulsory Voting

Do you support or oppose a law that would require all eligible citizens to vote in national elections and to impose a fine on eligible voters who do not have a good excuse for their failure to vote?

72%

21%

Oppose

Support

Percentage

Opinion

Mandatory Attendance at Polls Is Still Mandatory Voting

Ornstein was quick to point out that he doesn't necessarily support mandatory voting, but rather, in accordance with the system currently in place in Australia, "mandatory attendance at the polls." To me, this is just an attempt to deflect attention from the "mandatory" part. Poll "attendees" are still required to cast a ballot, and in Australia those who fail to do so—even if they showed up at the polls—can be prosecuted. Even choosing "none of the above" or "X," as is possible in Australia, involves casting a vote.

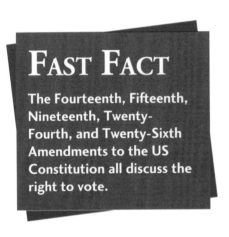

FAST FACT

The Fourteenth, Fifteenth, Nineteenth, Twenty-Fourth, and Twenty-Sixth Amendments to the US Constitution all discuss the right to vote.

Ornstein touted as a success the fact that, under Australia's compulsory system, only about three percent of voters write in "X." Meanwhile, in America, over 40 percent of eligible voters don't even go to the polls in any given election. So Australia is better off, right? If Ornstein's goal is to get only three percent of eligible American voters choosing "none of the above," then he will also have to deal with 37 percent of uninformed, disinterested, and apathetic Americans being forced to cast ballots for candidates about whom they know little, if anything at all. What good could come of that?

Consensus Is Not a Democratic Value

In his previous writings on the topic, Ornstein argues that mandatory voting will bring America to the center and eliminate the "polarizing" effect of partisan politics, especially in primary elections. His theory is that elective voting creates an environment where parties stir up their bases, leading to the election of increasingly more liberal Democrats and increasingly more conservative Republicans. With all of these radicals in office, he argues, "valuable Congressional time is spent on frivolous or narrow issues (flag burning, same-sex marriage) that are intended only to spur on the party bases and ideological extremes. Consequently, important, complicated issues (pension and health-care reform) get short shrift."

Although there are five constitutional amendments that mention the right to vote, the Constitution does not mention that voting is a civic duty.

Who decides which issues are important? Shouldn't politicians respond to what their constituents tell them is important? I chided Ornstein for trying to make everyone play "nice," as if politics could somehow lead to consensus through a utopian deliberative process. The Australian system he cites has not produced a placid political process by any means—and it's already been in use for decades.

Jury Duty and Voting Duty Serve Different Purposes

The most common argument put forth by supporters of compulsory voting is that, just as Americans have a civic obligation to perform jury duty, they should face a similar obligation to vote. This seems like a tempting argument, but it is based on a fundamentally flawed understanding of the Constitution and the Bill of Rights.

The Sixth and Seventh Amendments to the Constitution specify that both criminal and civil defendants have the right to a jury trial by their peers. For you to enjoy that right, your peers—and you in turn—must serve on a jury. This is one of the few instances where the Constitution compels citizens into service. There is no constitutional right to serve on the jury—it is a constitutional requirement on all voting citizens. This compelled service is correctly called a civic *duty*.

Voting is very different. No less than five constitutional amendments mention the right to vote, but nowhere in the Constitution is voting defined as a civic duty. As such, jury members are required to listen to both sides and then carefully deliberate before reaching a decision. Voters cannot be forced to listen to hours of campaign speeches before voting.

Most importantly, jury trials and elections serve different purposes in the American system of government. Juries act as a check on the power of the state, by shifting some of the judicial decision-making power to private citizens. Voting, by contrast, is the process by which citizens delegate power to government. Therefore, compulsory voting would entail forcing large numbers of people to make an uninformed decision on a matter of crucial importance.

Ornstein eventually conceded that compulsory voting would require "trivial" enforcement costs and would constitute a "trivial" loss of freedom. Yet the cumulative impact of past "trivial" costs has created today's huge budget deficit. And even "trivial" losses of freedoms over time move us in the direction of tyranny. Opinions may differ on whether greater voter turnout is a good thing, but no one should support policies designed to *force* people to be free.

EVALUATING THE AUTHOR'S ARGUMENTS:

In this viewpoint Fred L. Smith raises a concern about forcing uninformed voters to go to the polls. How do you think William A. Galston, author of the preceding viewpoint, would respond to this position?

Facts About the Election Process

Editor's note: These facts can be used in reports or papers to reinforce or add credibility when making important points or claims.

Federal Elections
- Congress has mandated a uniform date for presidential and congressional elections on Election Day, the Tuesday after the first Monday in November, or the Tuesday that falls on November 2 through November 8.
- Presidential elections take place every four years, and congressional elections take place every two years, with the congressional elections between presidential elections called "midterm elections."
- Members of the US Senate serve six-year terms, with one-third renewed every two years.
- Members of the US House of Representatives are elected for two-year terms.

State and Local Elections
- State legislatures regulate elections at the state and local levels.
- Elections for governor and other state offices are held at the same time as federal elections in most states except for Kentucky, Louisiana, Mississippi, New Jersey, and Virginia, which hold elections in odd-numbered years.

Electoral College
- Article II of the US Constitution specifies that the president and vice president of the United States shall be elected by electors from each state "equal to the whole Number of Senators and Representatives to which the State may be entitled in the Congress," known as the Electoral College.
- Under the Twenty-Third Amendment, Washington, DC, is allocated as many electors as it would have if it were a state, but no more electors than the least-populous state (currently three electors).

- The Electoral College consists of 538 electors, with the greatest number of electors from California, which has 55.
- The presidential candidate who receives the majority of electoral votes, at least 270, wins the presidency.
- All states except for Maine and Nebraska automatically award all electoral votes to the candidate who wins the popular vote in the state—the winner-take-all method.
- Maine and Nebraska use the congressional-district method, where the electoral votes are distributed based on the popular-vote winner within each congressional district, with the statewide popular-vote winner receiving two additional electoral votes.
- According to a 2011 Gallup Poll, 62 percent of Americans want to amend the US Constitution to replace the current electoral-college system with a nationwide popular-vote system.

Voter Eligibility and Registration
- Only US citizens are eligible to vote in US elections.
- The Fifteenth Amendment, adopted in 1870, prohibits any US citizen from being denied the right to vote on account of race, thereby extending the right to vote to African Americans.
- The Nineteenth Amendment, adopted in 1920, prohibits any US citizen from being denied the right to vote on account of sex, thereby extending the right to vote to women.
- The Twenty-Sixth Amendment to the US Constitution, adopted in 1971, set the minimum voting age at eighteen.
- All states, except for Maine and Vermont, deny incarcerated individuals the right to vote. Fourteen states prohibit anyone with a felony conviction from voting again, even after being released from prison.
- Every state except North Dakota requires that eligible voters register in order to vote.
- The National Voter Registration Act of 1993, also known as the Motor Voter Act, requires state governments to allow eligible voters to register to vote when they renew their driver's licenses or apply for social services.

Voter Turnout and Registration

According to the US Census Bureau:

- 57.1 percent of the voting-age population cast votes in the 2008 presidential election;
- In presidential elections since 1932, voter turnout was lowest in 1996, at 49 percent of the voting-age population, and highest in 1960, at 62.8 percent;
- 59.8 percent of the voting-age population was registered to vote in November 2010, but only 41.8 percent voted in the midterm elections that month.

Campaign Spending

According to the US Federal Election Commission:

- Over $1.6 billion was spent on the presidential race in 2008;
- Successful candidate Barack Obama spent the most money in 2008: $747.8 million;
- US House of Representative candidates spent over $1.1 billion in the 2009–2010 election cycle, and US Senate candidates spent over $755 million in that cycle.

Organizations to Contact

The editors have compiled the following list of organizations concerned with the issues debated in this book. The descriptions are derived from materials provided by the organizations. All have publications or information available for interested readers. The list was compiled on the date of publication of the present volume; the information provided here may change. Be aware that many organizations take several weeks or longer to respond to inquiries, so allow as much time as possible for the receipt of requested materials.

American Enterprise Institute for Public Policy Research (AEI)
1150 Seventeenth St. NW, Washington, DC 20036
(202) 862-5800 • fax: (202) 862-7177
e-mail: info@aei.org
website: www.aei.org

The AEI is a private, nonpartisan, nonprofit institution dedicated to research and education on issues of government, politics, economics, and social welfare. AEI sponsors research and publishes materials toward the end of defending the principles and improving the institutions of American freedom and democratic capitalism. AEI publishes the *American*, an online magazine; research papers; and its AEI Outlook series.

American National Election Studies (ANES)
Center for Political Studies, PO Box 1248, Ann Arbor, MI 48106-1248
(734) 764-5494 • fax: (734) 764-3341
e-mail: anes@electionstudies.org
website: www.electionstudies.org

The ANES is a collaboration of Stanford University and the University of Michigan that conducts national surveys of the American electorate and conducts development work through pilot studies. ANES produces data from its own surveys on voting, public opinion, and political participation. ANES provides data at its website through *ANES Guide*, a guide to public opinion and electoral behavior containing data from 1948 through 2008.

Americans Elect
PO Box 27875, Washington, DC 20038-7875
(541) 933-5328
e-mail: info@americanselect.org
website: www.americanselect.org

Americans Elect is a nonpartisan, nonprofit organization that is not affiliated with any political party, ideology, or candidate. Americans Elect has created the first nonpartisan presidential nomination online, aimed at putting a nonpartisan ticket on the 2012 presidential ballot. The organization has information about the nomination process, news, and videos available on its website.

Brookings Institution
1775 Massachusetts Ave. NW, Washington, DC 20036
(202) 797-6000
e-mail: communications@brookings.edu
website: www.brookings.edu

The Brookings Institution is a nonprofit public policy organization that conducts independent research. The institution uses its research to provide recommendations that advance the goals of strengthening American democracy, fostering social welfare and security, and securing a cooperative international system. The Brookings Institution publishes a variety of books, reports, and several journals.

Campaign Finance Institute (CFI)
1667 K St. NW, Ste. 650, Washington, DC 20006
(202) 969-8890 • fax: (202) 969-5612
e-mail: info@cfinst.org
website: www.cfinst.org

The CFI is a nonprofit, nonpartisan think tank for campaign finance policy. The institute provides analyses of election fund-raising, studies about the way interest groups spend money politically, and policy recommendations on effective disclosure. Available on its website are tables, charts, and data about campaign finance for both federal and state elections.

Campaign Legal Center

215 E St. NE, Washington, DC 20002
(202) 736-2200 • fax: (202) 736-2222
e-mail: info@campaignlegalcenter.org
website: www.campaignlegalcenter.org

The Campaign Legal Center is a nonpartisan, nonprofit organization that works in the areas of campaign finance and elections, political communication, and government ethics. The center offers nonpartisan analyses of issues and represents the public interest in administrative, legislative, and legal proceedings. The Campaign Legal Center publishes the *Legal Center Weekly Report*, available on its website, along with links to court cases and articles of interest.

Cato Institute

1000 Massachusetts Ave. NW, Washington, DC 20001
(202) 842-0200 • fax: (202) 842-3490
website: www.cato.org

The Cato Institute is a libertarian public policy research foundation dedicated to limiting the role of government, protecting individual liberties, and promoting free markets. The Cato Institute's economic research explores the benefits of lower taxes, a significantly reduced federal budget, and less government involvement in market processes. Among the institute's publications is the policy analysis "A Critique of the National Popular Vote."

Center for Competitive Politics (CCP)

124 S. West St., Ste. 201, Alexandria, VA 22314
(703) 894-6800 • fax: (703) 894-6811
e-mail: adickerson@campaignfreedom.org
website: www.campaignfreedom.org

The CCP works to promote and defend the First Amendment political rights of speech, assembly, and petition. It opposes efforts to limit campaign contributions, taxpayer-funded political campaigns, the "fairness doctrine" in talk radio, and other limits on the ability to support candidates and causes of one's choice. The center publishes research, which is available on its website, including "Issue Toolkit: Corporate Governance and Campaign Finance."

Center for Responsive Politics

1101 Fourteenth St. NW, Ste. 1030, Washington, DC 20005-5635
(202) 857-0044 • fax: (202) 857-7809
e-mail: info@crp.org
website: www.opensecrets.org

The Center for Responsive Politics tracks money in US politics and its effect on elections and public policy. It aims to inform and empower citizens by providing a resource for information about campaign contributions and lobbying. Available on the center's website is detailed information about the influence of money on elections, including a database of specific donor information.

Common Cause

1133 Nineteenth St. NW, 9th Fl., Washington, DC 20036
(202) 833-1200
website: www.commoncause.org

Common Cause promotes honest, open, and accountable government and encourages citizen participation in the functioning of US government. It leads campaigns for campaign finance reform, ethics and accountability in government, and reduced barriers to voting. Common Cause publishes reports on election policies, available on its website.

FairVote

6930 Carroll Ave., Ste. 610, Takoma Park, MD 20912
(301) 270-4616 • fax: (301) 270-4133
e-mail: info@fairvote.org
website: www.fairvote.org

FairVote is a national organization focused on fundamental structural reform of American elections. The organization works to promote fair access to participation in democracy, fair elections, and fair representation. FairVote has numerous research reports, policy perspectives, and democracy innovations available on its website, including "Federal Primary Runoff Elections and Voter Turnout Declines, 1994–2010."

Federal Election Commission (FEC)

999 E St. NW, Washington, DC 20463
(800) 424-9530
website: www.fec.gov

The FEC is an independent regulatory agency that administers and enforces the Federal Election Campaign Act (FECA), the statute that governs the financing of federal elections. The duties of the FEC are to disclose campaign finance information, to enforce provisions of the law such as the limits and prohibitions on contributions, and to oversee the public funding of presidential elections. The FEC has publications that explain the requirements of the federal campaign finance law, among other publications on the topic of federal elections.

Heritage Foundation
214 Massachusetts Ave. NE, Washington, DC 20002-4999
(202) 546-4400 • fax: (202) 546-8328
e-mail: info@heritage.org
website: www.heritage.org

The Heritage Foundation is a conservative public policy organization dedicated to promoting policies that align with the principles of free enterprise, limited government, individual freedom, traditional American values, and a strong national defense. The foundation conducts research on policy issues for members of Congress, key congressional staff members, policy makers in the executive branch, the nation's news media, and the academic and policy communities. The Heritage Foundation has hundreds of reports, fact sheets, testimonies, and commentaries available on its website.

Hoover Institution
434 Galvez Mall, Stanford University, Stanford, CA 94305-6010
(650) 723-1754
website: www.hoover.org

The Hoover Institution on War, Revolution, and Peace is a public policy research center devoted to advanced study of politics, economics, and political economy. The institution aims to be a contributor to the world marketplace of ideas defining a free society. The Hoover Institution publishes *Hoover Digest* and *Policy Review*, among other journals and books.

League of Women Voters
1730 M St. NW, Ste. 1000, Washington, DC 20036-4508
(202) 429-1965 • fax: (202) 429-0854
website: www.lwv.org

The League of Women Voters is a citizens' organization that works to improve government and engage all citizens in the decisions that impact their lives. Formed from the movement that secured the right to vote for women, the centerpiece of the League of Women Voters' efforts remain the expansion of participation and the giving of a voice to all Americans. Its website contains information about its efforts to improve elections and government and to educate and register voters.

National Popular Vote
Box 1441, Los Altos, CA 94023
(650) 472-1587 • fax: (650) 941-9430
e-mail: info@nationalpopularvote.com
website: www.nationalpopularvote.com

National Popular Vote is a nonprofit corporation working to implement a nationwide popular election of the president of the United States. National Popular Vote studies, analyzes, and educates the public regarding its proposal for a national popular vote. Available on its website are editorials and reports about the national popular vote alternative to the current Electoral College system.

Project Vote
737½ Eighth St. SE, Washington DC, 20003
(888) 546-4173
website: www.projectvote.org

Project Vote is a national nonpartisan, nonprofit organization that works to empower, educate, and mobilize low-income, minority, youth, and other marginalized and underrepresented voters. Project Vote has developed state-of-the-art voter registration and Get-Out-the-Vote programs and has helped register more than 5.6 million Americans in low-income and minority communities. Available on its website are publications on topics such as early voting, mail voting, voter fraud, and youth voting.

Rock the Vote
1001 Connecticut Ave. NW, Ste. 640, Washington, DC 20036
(202) 719-9910
website: www.rockthevote.com

Rock the Vote's mission is to engage and build political power for young people in the United States. The organization is dedicated to building the political power and clout of the "millennial generation" by registering and turning out young voters, by forcing the candidates to campaign to them, and by making politicians pay attention to youth and the issues they care about once in office. Available on its website are polls of young voters and information about the election process, including how to register to vote.

For Further Reading

Books

Abramson, Paul R., John H. Aldrich, and David W. Rohde. *Change and Continuity in the 2008 and 2010 Elections.* Washington, DC: CQ Press, 2011. Analyzes the 2008 and 2010 elections and the National Election Study surveys, presenting election data in a straightforward manner.

Alvarez, R. Michael, Thad E. Hall, and Susan D. Hyde, eds. *Election Fraud: Detecting and Deterring Electoral Manipulation.* Washington, DC: Brookings Institution, 2008. Presents research by leading scholars of election law, election administration, and US and comparative politics on defining, measuring, and detecting election fraud and electoral manipulation.

Balz, Dan, and Haynes Johnson. *The Battle for America: The Story of an Extraordinary Election.* New York: Penguin, 2010. Presents a nonpartisan account of the historic presidential election of 2008, offering a picture of the strategies and personalities of the candidates.

Fund, John H. *Stealing Elections: How Voter Fraud Threatens Our Democracy.* Revised and updated. New York: Encounter, 2008. Argues that US election systems are prone to error and plagued by incompetence and fraud, and discusses anomalies in past elections.

Goodman, Susan E. *See How They Run: Campaign Dreams, Election Schemes, and the Race to the White House.* New York: Bloomsbury, 2012. Explains the presidential election process from campaigning to the Electoral College system.

Keyssar, Alexander. *The Right to Vote: The Contested History of Democracy in the United States.* Rev. ed. New York: Basic Books, 2009. Recounts the evolution of suffrage from the American Revolution to the end of the twentieth century and explores the meaning of democracy in contemporary American life.

Minnite, Lorraine C. *The Myth of Voter Fraud.* Ithaca, NY: Cornell University Press, 2010. Presents the results of research looking for evidence of voter fraud, concluding that incidents of deliberate voter fraud are rare.

Overton, Spencer. *Stealing Democracy: The New Politics of Voter Suppression.* New York: Norton, 2007. Argues that elected officials and bureaucrats control thousands of election practices—from district boundaries to English-only ballots—that determine political winners and losers.

Pearlman, Nathaniel G., ed. *Margin of Victory: How Technologists Help Politicians Win Elections.* Santa Barbara, CA: Praeger, 2012. Discusses modern political technology, putting recent innovations into historical context and describing the possible future uses of technology in electoral politics.

Polsby, Nelson W., Aaron Wildavsky, Steven E. Schier, and David A. Hopkins. *Presidential Elections: Strategies and Structures of American Politics.* 13th ed. Lanham, MD: Rowman & Littlefield, 2011. Offers a complete overview of the presidential election process from the earliest straw polls and fund-raisers to final voter turnout and exit interviews.

Raymond, Allen. *How to Rig an Election: Confessions of a Republican Operative.* New York: Simon & Schuster, 2008. Gives a personal perspective on campaigning from a former Republican presidential campaign operative who ended up in prison.

Sides, John, Daron Shaw, Matt Grossman, and Keena Lipsitz. *Campaigns & Elections: Rules, Reality, Strategy, and Choice.* New York: Norton, 2011. Analyzes elections at the presidential, congressional, state, and local levels using a framework to illuminate the strategies and choices involved in American campaigns and elections.

Thurber, James A., and Candice J. Nelson, eds. *Campaigns and Elections American Style.* 3rd ed. Boulder, CO: Westview, 2009. Describes the innovation and reality of election campaigns as they have evolved over time to culminate in the phenomena of the new town meetings, bus tours, talk radio, infomercials, focus groups, and the Internet.

Traister, Rebecca. *Big Girls Don't Cry: The Election That Changed Everything for American Women.* New York: Simon & Schuster, 2010. Explores the role of women in the 2008 presidential election—from Hillary Clinton, to Sarah Palin, to women in the media—arguing that ultimately the election was good for women.

Wayne, Stephen J. *Is This Any Way to Run a Democratic Election?* 4th ed. Washington, DC: CQ Press, 2010. Discusses challenges in the American election system, including the demise of public funding, the use of new media, and changing sources of election news.

Periodicals and Internet Sources

Amira, Dan. "Why You Shouldn't Be Voting Today," *New York*, November 2, 2010.

Bennett, Robert. "Pros and Cons of Electoral College," *Deseret News* (Salt Lake City, UT), October 3, 2011.

Berman, Ari. "The GOP War on Voting," *Rolling Stone*, August 30, 2011.

Brannon, Ike. "The Upside of Voter ID Initiatives," *American*, June 16, 2011. www.american.com.

Brooks, David. "Don't Follow the Money," *New York Times*, October 19, 2010.

Carney, Eliza Newlin. "Is Now Really the Time to Loosen Corporate Spending?," *National Journal*, February 16, 2011.

Cutler, Eliot. "Who Stole Election Day?," *Wall Street Journal*, November 17, 2010.

Dionne, E.J., Jr. "How States Are Rigging the 2012 Election," *Washington Post*, June 19, 2011.

Dorf, Michael C. "The Supreme Court Rejects a Limit on Corporate-Funded Campaign Speech," FindLaw.com, January 25, 2010. www.findlaw.com.

Duke, Selwyn. "The Democrats' Final Recourse: Massive Voter Fraud," *American Thinker*, October 28, 2010. www.americanthinker.com.

Ferrara, Peter. "Voter Fraud," *American Spectator*, October 22, 2008. www.spectator.org.

Goldstein, Thomas C., and Amy Howe. "Bringing US Closer to a Real Democracy," *Politico*, April 19, 2011. www.politico.com.

Hall, Jon N. "Voter Fraud for the Complete Idiot," *American Thinker*, December 11, 2011. www.americanthinker.com.

Healy, Gene. "Stop Public Financing of Campaigns," *Washington Examiner*, February 15, 2011.

Hentoff, Nat. "Can Free Speech Be Redistributed?," Cato Institute, May 22, 2010. www.cato.org.

Holman, Rhonda. "Waiting for Evidence," *Wichita (KS) Eagle*, March 2, 2011.

Investor's Business Daily. "Denying Our Soldiers the Vote," September 24, 2010.

Jacoby, Jeff. "The 'Big Dog' in Campaign Spending," *Boston Globe*, October 31, 2010.

Kilgore, Ed. "The Truth About Voter Suppression," *Salon*, September 30, 2011. www.salon.com.

Law, Steven J. "Organized Labor and *Citizens United*," *Wall Street Journal*, March 10, 2010.

Leval, Jessica, and Jennifer Marsico, "The Rise of 'Convenience Voting,'" *American*, October 16, 2008. www.american.com.

Leval, Jessica M. "Make Absentee Voting Easier for Military Members," *Roll Call*, January 22, 2009.

Levy, Robert A. "Confusing the Cost of Free Speech," *Washington Times*, August 10, 2010.

Lewiston (ID) Morning Tribune. "Editorial: Why Washington Votes and Idaho Doesn't," November 30, 2010.

Malkin, Michelle. "The Left's Voter-Fraud Whitewash," *National Review Online*, October 27, 2010. www.nationalreview.com.

Miller, Matt. "How Billionaires Could Save the Country," *Washington Post*, August 31, 2011.

Nation. "Curbing Campaign Cash," June 6, 2011.

New York Times. "The Myth of Voter Fraud," October 9, 2011.

Ornstein, Norman J. "Got More Voters? Get More Electoral Votes," *New York Times*, November 17, 2011.

Ornstein, Norman J., and Thomas E. Mann. "Pitfalls of a Third-Party Candidacy," *Washington Post*, September 14, 2011.

Parnell, Sean, and Matthew Nese. "Do Lower Contribution Limits Produce 'Good' Government?," Center for Competitive Politics, July 2011. www.campaignfreedom.org.

Richwine, Jason. "Abolish Recounts," *National Review Online*, January 29, 2009. www.nationalreview.com.

Roanoke (VA) Times. "Make It Easier to Vote," November 26, 2010.

Samples, John. "The First Amendment Guarantees the *Citizens United* Decision," *US News and World Report*, September 27, 2010.

Samples, John. "Leave Electoral College Intact," *Nashville Tennessean*, March 9, 2011.

Singer, Peter. "Why Vote?," Project Syndicate, December 14, 2007. www.project-syndicate.org.

Smith, Bradley A. "The Myth of Campaign Finance Reform," *National Affairs*, Winter 2010.

Soros, Jonathan. "It's Time to Junk the Electoral College," *Wall Street Journal*, December 14, 2008.

Steiger, Kay. "Another State Targets Phantom Voter Fraud," *American Prospect*, January 25, 2011. www.prospect.org.

Taylor, Paul W. "Why Hasn't Voting by Mail Spread?," *Governing*, March 2011.

Thiessen, Marc A. "In Defense of the GOP Debates," *Washington Post*, October 31, 2011.

Trzupek, Rich. "Voter Fraud in America," *FrontPage*, October 29, 2010. www.frontpagemag.com.

Von Spakovsky, Hans. "Destroying the Electoral College: The Anti-federalist National Popular Vote Scheme," *Legal Memorandum*, October 27, 2011. www.heritage.org.

Von Spakovsky, Hans. "Elections Exclusively by Mail: A Terrible Idea Whose Time Should Never Come," *Legal Memorandum*, April 21, 2010. www.heritage.org

Wang, Tova Andrea. "Voter Fraud Hysteria," *Politico*, November 1, 2010. www.politico.com.

Wilkinson, Will. "Thank You for Not Voting," *Ottawa (ON) Citizen*, October 22, 2008.

Willoughby, Nikki. "DISCLOSE Act Is an Opening, Not a Barrier," Cato Unbound, November 12, 2010. www.cato-unbound.org.

Woolington, Rebecca. "What's Wrong with Early Voting?," *Portland Oregonian*, October 13, 2011.

Websites

ElectionLine.org (www.electionline.org). This website provides a non-partisan, nonadvocacy information clearinghouse and e-newsletter with news and analysis on election reform.

National Conference on State Legislatures (www.ncsl.org). This website has information about state elections, state election laws and procedures, and state election results.

US Election Assistance Commission (www.eac.gov). This website contains resources for voters such as the National Mail Voter Registration Form, information on voting system testing, and voting research and data.

Index

upholds voter identification laws, 15

was correct to overturn limits on corporate campaign advertising, 46–51

Surveys

amending Constitution to provide for direct election of president, 92

application of campaign finance laws equally to corporations/unions/ individuals, 66

campaign donations as form of free speech, *67*

Citizens United decision, *55*

influence of money in elections, 2010, *62, 62–63*

prevalence of blacks voting early in Georgia, 36

prohibition of political ads, *75*

support for mandatory voting, US, *109*

support of requiring photo IDs at polling places, *83*

voting by ineligible voters as major problem, *31*

Twenty-Fourth Amendment, 110

Twenty-Sixth Amendment, 110

Unions

Citizens United decision on political spending by, 8, 49

DISCLOSE Act exemptions for, 76

efforts in Wisconsin to limit influence of, 61–62

limits on political spending by, 9

opinions on restrictions on political advertising by, *75*

US Constitution, 107

Amendments dealing with right to vote in, 110, 112

percentage of Americans willing to amend to allow for direct election of president, 92

See also specific amendments

USA Today (newspaper), 28

Valeo, Buckley v. (1976), 8

Von Spakovsky, Hans A., 13, 80

Voter fraud

efforts to prevent are not racist, 27–32

efforts to prevent discriminate against minorities, 21–26

evidence shows concerns about, are unfounded, 16–20

is problem affecting fair elections, 11–15

risk of, in absentee voting, 43–44

voter ID laws can help prevent, 81–82

Voter ID cards, *17, 79*

Voter identification

should be required, 80–84

should not be required, 85–90

Voter identification laws, states enacting, in 2011, 87

Voter registration fraud, federal prosecutions of, 2002–2005, *19*

Picture Credits

© AP Images, 23

© AP Images/Chattanooga Times Free Press/Jake Daniels, 81

© AP Images/Mike Derer, 93

© AP Images/Ric Feld, 17

© AP Images/Journal Times/Scott Anderson, 79

© AP Images/PR Newswire, 65

© AP Images/Erik Schelzig, 13

© AP Images/Dana Verkouteran, 48

© Bill Clark/CQ Roll Call/Getty Images, 56

© David R. Frazier Photolibrary, Inc./Alamy, 111

© Directphoto.org/Alamy, 37

Gale/Cengage Learning, 14, 19, 31, 50, 55, 62, 67, 75, 83, 94, 100, 104, 109

© Darren Hauck/Getty Images, 60

© Chris McGrath/ALLSPORT/Getty Images, 106

© Win McNamee/Getty Images, 45

© William B. Plowman/NBC/NBCU Photo Bank via Getty Images, 29

© Joe Raedle/Getty Images, 42

© Reuters/Landov, 98

© Chip Somodevilla/Getty Images, 71, 77

© Jim West/Alamy, 10

© David Young-Wolff/Alamy, 88

The election
process.

DATE			